CREATIVE GENIUS

GREAT MINDS SERIES BY PETER FRITZ WALTER

KRISHNAMURTI AND THE PSYCHOLOGICAL REVOLUTION

CREATIVE GENIUS: FOUR-QUADRANT CREATIVITY IN THE LIVES AND
WORKS OF LEONARDO DA VINCI, WILHELM REICH, ALBERT
EINSTEIN, SVJATOSLAV RICHTER AND KEITH JARRETT

FRITJOF CAPRA AND THE SYSTEMS VIEW OF LIFE

FRANÇOISE DOLTO AND CHILD PSYCHOANALYSIS

EDWARD DE BONO AND THE MECHANISM OF MIND

JOSEPH MURPHY AND THE POWER OF YOUR SUBCONSCIOUS MIND

JOSEPH CAMPBELL AND THE LUNAR BULL

TERENCE MCKENNA AND ETHNOPHARMACOLOGY

CHARLES W. LEADBEATER AND THE INNER LIFE

ANTONIO VILLOLDO AND HEALING THE LUMINOUS BODY

WILHELM REICH AND THE FUNCTION OF THE ORGASM

CREATIVE GENIUS

Four-Quadrant Creativity in the Lives and Works of Leonardo da Vinci, Wilhelm Reich, Albert Einstein, Svjatoslav Richter and Keith Jarrett

Short Biographies, Book and Media Reviews, Quotes, and Comments (Great Minds Series, Vol. 2)

By Peter Fritz Walter

Published by Sirius-C Media Galaxy LLC

113 Barksdale Professional Center, Newark, Delaware, USA

Set in Palatino

Designed by Peter Fritz Walter

ISBN 978–1–502819–0–31

Publishing Categories
Psychology / Creative Ability

Publisher Contact Information
publisher@sirius-c-publishing.com
http://sirius-c-publishing.com

Author Contact Information
pfw@peterfritzwalter.com

About Dr. Peter Fritz Walter
http://peterfritzwalter.com

About the Author

Parallel to an international law career in Germany, Switzerland and the United States, Dr. Peter Fritz Walter (Pierre) focused upon fine art, cookery, astrology, musical performance, social sciences and humanities.

He started writing essays as an adolescent and received a high school award for creative writing and editorial work for the school magazine.

After finalizing his law diplomas, he graduated with an LL.M. in European Integration at Saarland University, Germany, in 1982, and with a Doctor of Law title from University of Geneva, Switzerland, in 1987.

He then took courses in psychology at the University of Geneva and interviewed a number of psychotherapists in Lausanne and Geneva, Switzerland. His interest was intensified through a hypnotherapy with an Ericksonian American hypnotherapist in Lausanne. This led him to the recovery and healing of his inner child.

After a second career as a corporate trainer and personal coach, Pierre retired in 2004 as a full-time writer, philosopher and consultant.

His nonfiction books emphasize a systemic, holistic, cross-cultural and interdisciplinary perspective, while his fiction works and short stories focus upon education, philosophy, perennial wisdom, and the poetic formulation of an integrative worldview.

Pierre is a German-French bilingual native speaker and writes English as his 4th language after German, Latin and French. He also reads source literature for his research works in Spanish, Italian, Portuguese, and Dutch. In addition, Pierre has notions of Thai, Khmer, Chinese, Japanese, and Vietnamese.

All of Pierre's books are hand-crafted and self-published, designed by the author. Pierre publishes via his Delaware company, Sirius-C Media Galaxy LLC, and under the imprints of IPUBLICA and SCM (Sirius-C Media).

To all young geniuses of our day,

who have deserved to be recognized

The author's profits from this book are being donated to charity.

Contents

Chapter Four   195
The Genius of Svjatoslav Richter

Chapter Five   227
The Genius of Keith Jarrett

Bibliography   253
Contextual Bibliography

Personal Notes   277

The difference between stupidity and genius is that genius has its limits.

—ALBERT EINSTEIN

Introduction

The Spontaneous Nature of Life

All creation is effortless and spontaneous.

Einstein knew it. He woke up one morning, and had dreamt it all out. It was the day he made the first sketch for relativity theory. He had anticipated his breakthrough in a dream.

Creators anticipate their creation through insights from the unified field. They anticipate creation through *intuition*. That is what renders the creator distinct from the craftsman. The craftsman acts in alignment with the past, based upon conservative values, whereas the creator acts in the present, based upon new and alternative values.

Crafting needs effort, creating is effortless. If effort there is, it sets in *after* the basic creation, the prime creative idea. Then only, consistency is needed to carry the work through to its final achievement.

In the creative phase, however, there is chaos, not consistency, disorder, not order, and the constants of life are *reshuffled, retested, reaffirmed,* and if needed, *discarded.*

I got a hint of this as a student when, fascinated about the Russian-German pianist Svjatoslav Richter, I went to our local music store to get what I could of his records. He was the only exception to the rule I knew at the time, that is, I found Richter was an *artist and craftsman in one person;* he was aligned with conservative values and alternative values at the same time, thereby breaking the rule. When I listened to Richter, music became for me so plastic and dramatic that I thought there must be a relativity far beyond the one Einstein discovered, a relativity that is something like a law of relationships!

It was the *coherence* in his interpretations that triggered the idea in me. I over and over again wondered how the same music by the same composer could sound so different, plain and genuine with Richter, and fragmented, hollow and outlandish with a lesser gifted pianist?

Richter's craftsmanship, the immense authenticity of his musical diction and pianistic perfection, became for me a metaphor for the power of art. In my younger years, I felt more at home in the art universe than in the science world, so my attraction to Richter felt natural. My attraction to Einstein was of a more academic nature, initially. And yet, I had to admit that Einstein was the greater genius, for he was artist *and* scientist.

All creation sets novelty in place, a pattern of relationships—the invisible threads of potentiality woven into a different arrangement.

The surprise is that the pattern, though novel, looks familiar and one feels 'at home' in every new and great work of human genius. This is the very secret of genius; it always feels great and true, revolting—yet simple in its high complexity.

I was speechless most of the time when listening to Richter, especially in my younger years, and I would cry and weep when listening to certain favorite compositions of mine that he played with outstanding brilliance and grandeur—such as Rachmaninov's 2nd Piano Concerto, Prokofiev's Second Sonata, or Scriabin's op. 28 Fantasy.

I believe that quantum physics teaches us that art cannot be conventional, that it cannot, as

Krishnamurti would say, belong to the 'known.' When novelty is rendered conventional, it is no more novelty. When particles are unobserved, they are in a state of innocence. There are dancing with the universe, and are 'all over the place'—nonlocal. Means … , totally connected.

Only under the eyes of an observer, they localize and become entangled with the observer, thereby losing their joy of nonlocality. They become enamored with the one and only one, their observer! Why? Because of his attention. When my thoughts can impregnate the memory surface of water, they are creative! And by extension they can be destructive, depending on my intentionality.

Quantum physics thus is the secret behind all creation, behind all novelty, behind all genius. It is the matrix that explains the unlimited genius and creative force of the human mind! That in turn means that the quantum field as the creational matrix is our true belonging. We are not machines, but if ever, quantum machines, patterns of complex relationships aligning energy and information. We are vibrating crystals!

What is Creativity?

Human creativeness is a latent potentiality, while creativity is to be understood as the *practical realization* of this potentiality. As long as creativity is not realized, it is potentiality, and outside of space-time. When it is being realized, it makes its way into space-time, and crystallizes in particular talent, particular genius, which is always specific.

We all are potentially creative as humans, but most of us live with a dormant creativeness rather than an awake creativity. Contrary to Edward de Bono's idea of *serious creativity*, the 'deliberate effort of the mind to think different,' I believe that there is no effort in creativity, first of all.

Second, it is not thought that is creative, and can be creative, at all. It is the space in between thoughts which has the potential of creating novelty. It is when thought is not that we are truly creative. As Krishnamurti has amply explained, this is so because thought is always in the past. It is circular, it cannot create novelty, it can only endlessly repeat and reshuffle its content. In one word, and to repeat it, creativity is a faculty of *intuition*, not of thought.

Edward de Bono clarified from the start that his concept of *serious creativity* does not pertain to the creativity of the artist, but is valid for the corporate world; it could be termed 'business creativity.'

—See Peter Fritz Walter, Edward de Bono and the Mechanism of Mind (Great Minds Series, Vol. 5), 2015/2017.

That is why it is deliberate and based upon effort. I do not deny its effectiveness, but here I am talking about *general* creativity, which includes artistic creativity.

We all know that artists are creative. This is some of the things we already learnt in school. What we however did not learn, or most of us, is that *all humans are creative*, in the sense that genuine creativeness simply is a natural add-on to the human nature. You see that with children. All children are creative. Why are not all adults creative?

There are precise factors that make that human creativity, the practical day-to-day application of creativeness, is thwarted. It's like a muscle you never use; it gets weaker and weaker, and then one day, the muscle atrophies and becomes dysfunctional. Creativity is as it were the muscle of genuine creativeness; or we can say that creativity is the lens through which human creativeness sees its day and becomes visible in daily life. When we are not creative in the practical sense, let's say in finding new ways of doing, drafting new concepts or inventing new things, we are still creative humans, but our lacking creativity makes that our creativeness becomes stagnant.

Let me give some examples of genuinely creative people, who were able to channel their creativeness into serious or not so serious creativity. Let me tell you that this list is only the peak of the iceberg. I would like to mention here Pablo Picasso, Charles Chaplin, Albert Einstein, Nikola Tesla, Fritjof Capra, Edward de Bono, Dale Carnegie, Svjatoslav Richter, Herbert von Karajan, and Keith Jarrett.

These ten great men, three physicists, two think tanks and corporate coaches, and five artists, have displayed, and display, high creativity. When studying their life stories, their art, their musical performances, their concepts, their patents, we see that creativity is not limited to art or music, but displays its power as well in the corporate world, in business, and in the technical sphere.

This insight led me to distinguish four basic realms of creativity:

▸ Artistic Creativity

▸ Scientific Creativity

▸ Conceptual or Business Creativity

▸ Technical Creativity

Let me give some examples of each. When I look at *artistic creativity*, I see that Pablo Picasso (1881-1973) created modern art forms virtually from scratch that were nonexistent before. He ventured into realms of visual art that were so daring that many people, until Picasso was in old age, and world-famous, rejected his art as 'iconoclast vandalism,' 'childish immaturity' or 'deliberate ridicule.' With Charlie Chaplin (1889-1977) we see a man who already well-known as an actor, broke with tradition and his former role image, to create the figure of the street vamp and charming clown, virtually from rags and tatters found in his studio, and dared into the unknown. He was ridiculed at first, but finally became victorious after many trials.

When we look at *scientific creativity*, we see two men standing out, Albert Einstein (1879-1955), today recognized as a universal genius, brilliant physicist, mathematician and musician (violinist), and Nikola Tesla (1856-1943), controversial inventor, and creator of more than 400 patents on inventions. When we look at *conceptual or business creativity*, we could look at men like Dale Carnegie, Edward de Bono or else Sergio Zyman, who have changed our corporate world with their original and daring concepts.

Dale Carnegie (1888-1955) became the first internationally known life coach and corporate trainer and yet when he started out, he was unable to hold a speech in front of small audience, and learnt it all from the bottom up. He created major concepts for human resource training that today are no more reflected about, but taken for granted. This is even more so the case with Edward de Bono, born in 1933, so far in human history the greatest and most versatile life coach and corporate trainer, a think tank who has revolutionized the business world with his brilliant concepts and insights.

He is credited as the proprietor of 'lateral thinking,' the '6 Hats' brainstorming method, 'tactical' success training, conflicts solution, the 'six action shoes,' etc. With Sergio Zyman we have a business man and corporate leader who is a bit more controversial in that he stands out not only through his ruthlessness but also his concept-inventiveness when leading the *Coca Cola Company* to worldwide success. While he's a controversial figure, his overall creativity for concept-design cannot be overlooked for it stands out as an example for how to go beyond mere marketing and instead create lasting business success with 'deliberate concept design.' That it works, his successes have proven it.

Technical creativity is very important as well, and often visible in our media or fashion magazines. It's not only the creativity and solution thinking of an engineer, but also the daring creations of a couturier, interior designer, architect, car maker, perfume distiller or shoe maker.

This kind of creativity comes over as so spontaneous and natural that most people never even think about it. Yet it's an integral part of all cultures' aesthetic achievements and craftsmanship.

Genius and Inner Knowledge

We have seen above that *integrated knowledge* is quite something different than the ordinary knowledge traditional science used to consider. Integrated knowledge always existed because it is inner knowledge. We all possess it, but only men and women of genius use it to its fullest, thereby benefitting from universal and perhaps superhuman knowledge sources. Let me exemplify this with the art of learning the piano, and filmmaking.

When Charlie Chaplin started his fabulous career as a film comic, he used the simplest means, and much of it was improvised in the beginning. Chaplin was not interested in the ordinary roles that were offered to him by producers.

Deep down he knew that he owned more power and creativity than all those mediocre film producers. Charlie, the figure of the street vamp, clown and charming guy was created from rags and utensils that Chaplin spontaneously fit for costumes. If Charles had not followed his intuition and not played out his cards, Charlie would never have been born. Charlie was the ingenious Pygmalion of Charles.

All through my younger years, I studied biographies and autobiographies. Among the ones that fascinated me most was Charles Chaplin's autobiography.

—Charles Chaplin, My Autobiography, New York: Plume, 1992. First published in 1964.

I found he was unique because of his trusting his creative instinct, his own star—although at the decisive point in his life, when he began carrying out his first vision of Charlie, everything and everyone seemed to be against him.

We all have a tendency to look at famous and successful people only from the moment they made it, overlooking the many years of sacrifice and failure they have lived through *before* they were famous.

Edward de Bono, the leading think tank, has written an extraordinary book entitled *Tactics: The Art and Science of Success.*

—Edward de Bono: Tactics: The Art and Science of Success, London: HarperCollins, 1993, first published in 1985.

This book, which is based on the thorough human resource studies of Piers Dudgeon and Valerie Jennings, presents a precious pandora box full of tactical advice about how to become successful and gain fame. The study is based on fifty interviews with men and women who have been outstandingly successful, among them *David Bailey, Hans Eysenck, Malcolm Forbes, Clive Sinclair, Jackie Stewart* and *Virginia Wade.* With his usual lucidity Edward de Bono analyzes their different paths to success, revealing some striking truths such as 'Building your strengths brings you more success than compensating for your weaknesses' or 'People care is of huge importance in achieving success.'

The artist where I have seen inner knowledge as if under a magnifier is Pablo Picasso. Among all artists, I do not know one who enjoyed a similar independence and inventiveness. While his contemporaries, like Braque, tried to learn from his early cubism, Picasso in turn did not need to take anything from others. At age fourteen, he could paint like the classical masters, and it's notorious that his father gave up teaching him anything. His life was not easy once he left his home in Malaga, leaving behind a loving mother and a highly intelligent father, who was a well-known art teacher. Picasso went to leave Spain and settled in Paris, France, only a few years later.

It is also documented that when Braque and Picasso shared an apartment in Paris, when both were very poor, Picasso made a few canvasses in Braque's style, just for the fun of it all. Some experts believe they were better than Braque's originals. Anyway, it led to the break of the friendship because Braque could not live with the idea that his art was for Picasso nothing but child play.

You see in Picasso's art career that his fierce independence even became stronger as he grew older. To look only at *Guernica*, the monumental painting which assumed a unique expressiveness under Picasso's hands.

I do not know any other artwork that associates the senseless cruelty of war or civil war in such a sublimated abstract form, unveiling the misery of misguided humanity without itself containing the violence a realistic painting or photography would depict. You can contemplate *Guernica* and be deeply moved, without being sickened. In this sense, *Guernica* is a cathartic experience, and was so for Picasso himself.

From about the time Picasso lived in the Chateau de Vauvenargues, with Jacqueline at his side, his art became so unique and personal, without any possible comparison with existing models, that even some Picasso lovers felt estranged. Picasso was using his inner knowledge once again to a point to use it as an exclusive inspiration for his art.

I believe that there is a similarly gigantic originality with the pianist Svjatoslav Richter. While still some decades ago, many doubted that musical performance involves real creativity, this point has been clarified. I remember that back in the 1960s this discussion was still vivid, while today most art critics and even the lay public have accepted the idea that musical performance can be *genuinely creative.* That doesn't imply however that it always is, but it potentially can be.

Back in my childhood, I saw this discussion engaged in Germany regarding Herbert von Karajan, Glenn Gould and Svjatoslav Richter. In the performances of these three artists, a conductor and two pianists, critics and a growing part of the public began to voice things like 'recomposition,' 'recreation,' 'remodeling the original composition,' 'co-creating the original,' and so on. It was Karajan's *Mahler,* Glenn Gould's *Bach* and Richter's *Rachmaninov* that triggered the peak of this discussion about musical aesthetics and right-or-wrong interpretation of a musical composition.

It is curious to see today that these positions have not changed over time. Still now, most critics, and even a new generation of them, say that Karajan was best in Mahler, Gould in Bach and Richter in Rachmaninov. Richter who did not particularly like Karajan, admitted in his Notebooks about Karajan that, 'his Mahler is great.' Richter recreated the Rachmaninov image to a point of no-return; later in life, he did the same with Schubert. As he relates in *Richter the Enigma (1998):*

> Everybody asked me why I wanted to play Schubert? It's Schumann you have to play, not Schubert, they said, but I did not listen. I *knew* I wanted to play Schubert, however differently!

—Richter The Enigma / L'Insoumis / Der Unbeugsame, NVC Arts 1998 (DVD).

I think this is a particularly striking example of how a great artist uses his inner knowledge or pure intuition to venture into avenues unknown to millions of people over generations and generations! The service that Richter has rendered Schubert is not to express in words, so precious and unprecedented it is, as he was never understood, overshadowed at his lifetime by Beethoven, and forgotten for more than a century after his death. Richter showed the world that

Schubert's sonatas stand on equal foot, both in form and in expression, with Beethoven's. This is particularly true for his long B-flat Major Sonata.

Glenn Gould speaks in an interview about it, saying he struggled with the 'repetitive structures' of the sonata and became restless and squirmy when he had to sit through it. And that when he saw Richter playing it in Moscow Conservatory, back in the 1950s, it was like a veil was lifted before his eyes and he suddenly understood that all repetitions were 'organic elements' in the musical piece and that despite the fact that Richter seemed to play the sonata slower than all pianists he had heard playing it before, all seemed to be right in place, and that he had been captivated from the first to the last note.

—Richter The Enigma / L'Insoumis / Der Unbeugsame, NVC Arts
1998 (DVD).

Gould, talking with so much true reverence about
Richter, was a musical genius himself. Gifted just as
Richter with a *photographic memory*, he was never once
seen to play from a score, while even Richter later in
life doubted his fantastic memory when playing in
public.

Gould has left us a Bach that *sings*. When the
transition came from playing Bach on a harpsichord
to playing him on a modern concert grand, most
pianists, to this day, have a tendency to play Bach
without pedal, using so-called 'finger technique' to
render a Bach that strangely reminds of Clementi,
Czerny and Hanon, instead of reminding of Bach.

I still remember that when I heard Bach on the
radio in my childhood, I found his music 'hard and
violent,' and thought it was bare of emotion and of
tender feelings. Then you listen to the *Well-Tempered
Clavier* or the *French Suites* in our days, with Richter,
Perahia or Gavrilov, and you realize that the world
has changed.

Bach, in fact, contains more tenderness than
Telemann and Handel, only that pianists have
discovered it rather late. Already the Russian pianist

Heinrich Neuhaus, the teacher of Svjatoslav Richter and Emil Gilels, wrote in his book *The Art of Piano Playing* that a pianist can play Bach only if he is able to let 'every single voice' sing.

—Heinrich Neuhaus, The Art of Piano Playing, London: Barrie & Jenkins, 1973, first published in 1958.

But as I said earlier, it is well a difference to do something about musical performance because it is recognized by an authority, or to do it because of a strong inner voice that says 'Do it'! So let us explore now how this is possible at all, how we can have sure inner knowledge about things to come or things we should realize, while the whole world sees matters differently, and tells us to do things in the old ways?

I believe that quantum physics and especially the principles of *uncertainty* and *nonlocality* provide the answers that are not answered since the times of Leonardo da Vinci.

Four-Quadrant Genius

Geniuses, in the past, and today, are geniuses not because they attended schools and universities, but *despite* having done so. What is characteristic about them is that they know better than their teachers and generally suffer from the restrictions and limitations inherent in any school system. In addition, it has not been understood until recently that human intelligence is not uniform in the sense that not every genius is a genius in all four quadrants, nor in just one of them. This model is of course a simplification. Einstein's genius wasn't just 1st quadrant: deductive-logical-analytical. He said that he arrived at none of his discoveries *'through rational thinking.'* It is that his right-brain intelligence was especially strong, the 2nd quadrant: holistic-intuitive-integrative intelligence.

Generally speaking, my point is that genius is genius not because any quadrant of their IQ is especially highly developed, but because there is an extraordinary *systemic reinforcement* of the general IQ through the *synergy* between different modes of intelligence.

For example, in Einstein's case, and even more so, in Leonardo's case, the 1st and the 2nd quadrant IQ were adding-on to one another with the result of an extraordinary lucidity that is able to check back any little progress in *analysis* with an equal progress in *synthesis*. A wise man once stated that after psychoanalysis must come *psychosynthesis*. I am convinced that if Roberto Assagioli had not invented the latter, another would have done so, simply because it was the lacking half. In fact, if tomorrow you invent another alphabet and you write its first letter, A, you cannot stay there, but you must get through until Z. Only when A to Z is finalized, you can say you have the basis of a coherent something that you call a *language*.

When research on brain hemispheres was developed, the first insight, revolutionary at the time, was that IQ is proportionally higher in case of a *coherence between the brain hemispheres*. This produced the long-overdue insight that genius is not, as formerly believed, an extraordinary development of one of the IQ quadrants, but rather an unusual equilibrium of the left and right brain hemispheres that leads to what could be called an *integrated* thought process.

This implies that conscious and subconscious mind work in sync, and for this, we have many examples in the lives of highly gifted people. Einstein, for example, used to have little naps throughout the day, short periods when he fell asleep, for no longer than about ten minutes, and sometimes, after waking up, he intuitively felt he had found the solution to one or the other hairy scientific problem he was working on.

In this context, it is helpful to study the various tests that were conducted on Einstein's brain after his death. It was found that his brain did not display abnormalities or hypertrophies of any kind: it was found to be a 'normal brain' in every respect. Some people, who had expected to find 'the key to Einstein's genius' were disappointed in their hope to detect the one single key to human genius, so that it could be cloned.

The answer is that there is no such key, except that geniuses seem to use their brains way more efficiently than ordinary people do.

I actually researched this matter but found that not even the legal questions are free of doubt, let alone the various theories about Einstein's brain. In some books it's written he had agreed by testamentary will that his brain was given to research after his death, but in others, it was said that he had expressed his last will only verbally.

Fact is that his son, Hans Albert Einstein, had to give an ex-post permission to the autopsy, which is legally a hairy case by itself.

In fact, we know from research that most people use only five to eight percent of their creative resources, but geniuses definitely use more; how much more is still not entirely clarified and subject to further research. I am convinced that all in life is linked through feedback-cycles, a fact now corroborated by systems theory. In high achievers we can observe a *reinforcing cycle* put in place by the very fact of their own belief in being superior!

The will to achieve higher sets in place an evolutionary upward spiral that positively affects the development of the brain and the building of *preferred pathways*, thereby raising the complexity of neuronal connections.

Salvador Dali (1904-1989) is a stunning example as he had taken the decision as a little boy to be a genius; he relates that in his notebooks. It is not surprising, then, that later in life, while not without hassles, he was recognized as an artistic genius.

Whatever may be true in this respect, there is no doubt that high self-confidence, and a high level of trust in life is conducive to achieving higher, for outperforming oneself, and for delivering outstanding achievements.

Françoise Dolto (1908-1988) related to me in an interview that at the critical moments in her life when she was developing her famed method for healing psychotic children, she felt she was 'walking on eggs' and did not feel she knew what was going on. It has to be known that at that time, it was believed that psychosis is a fatal disease and cannot be healed, be it manifest in a child or an adult. It was even believed that in every case of psychosis a physical brain damage is the root cause. Today we know that all this is not true, but these new insights still haven't reached popular science circles.

What happened to Dolto was that she fell asleep in a therapy session with a psychotic child. She didn't understand at first why this was so, but it seemed to be so compelling that she later used to say that psychotic children *get their therapist in trance.'* She then found out that the child's psyche actually asked for a *non-biased direct communicative link* with the therapist, which ideally comes about telepathically, when the therapist's reasoning mind is put at rest for a moment. And to her great astonishment, she found that every time after a session she had fallen asleep with a psychotic child, that child had done a major leap forward in healing the disturbance.

With Françoise Dolto, I had found a particularly striking example for the fact that genius also requires a very high level of trust in inner guidance.

When Einstein published his *Annus Mirabilis Papers* in 1905, his work on the essence of radiation in 1909, and his ground-breaking study on the theory of relativity in 1915, the scientific world ignored them at first. Nobody saw what a revolution had happened in science with the emergence of these papers, simply because there was nobody who was able to evaluate them in the first place. It was only from 1919, because astronomers had confirmed Einstein's prediction of gravitational reflection of starlight by the Sun during a solar eclipse in Brazil that Einstein got the merits he deserved for his discoveries. But Einstein himself, like Dolto, never had doubted that what he discovered had prime value; he most probably did not a moment worry about fame or recognition but simply continued his work. He also could not be sure, at that time, just like Dolto, that what he found was really going to be fully verified as a theory.

We know that in the short intervals before falling asleep and right after waking up, we are in the so-called *alpha* state, which is when brain waves are somewhat longer than in the 'thinking' state of full awareness, and it is in this state that the brain hemispheres are particularly in sync. This means that the *corpus callosum*, the structure that connects the brain hemispheres in the mammalian brain, is especially active.

In fact, all of the inter-hemispheric communication in the brain is conducted across the *corpus callosum*. This is why, as Einstein used to say, a problem cannot be solved on the same level of thought that created it. In other words, solving problems is not possible through logical deductive thinking, which is left-brain related, but must involve in addition inductive and associative thinking, which is right-brain related. Interestingly so, Einstein himself did not talk about his genius in the usual terms. He was way more specific. He used to say that contrary to most other scientists he was extremely stubborn (*starrköpfig*), and, facing a problem, he would react to it with 'dogged endurance.'

Another great genius, Johann Wolfgang von Goethe (1749-1832), said that genius is diligence *(Genie ist Fleiss)*. Einstein also said that 'the gift of fantasy' has meant more to him than effort done for absorbing 'positive knowledge.'

In Einstein's case, we clearly see that it was these qualities of the right brain, including imagination, fantasy, the capacity to see hidden connections between obvious appearances, and musical talent that made for his astounding discoveries in atomic physics.

Chapter One

The Genius of Leonardo

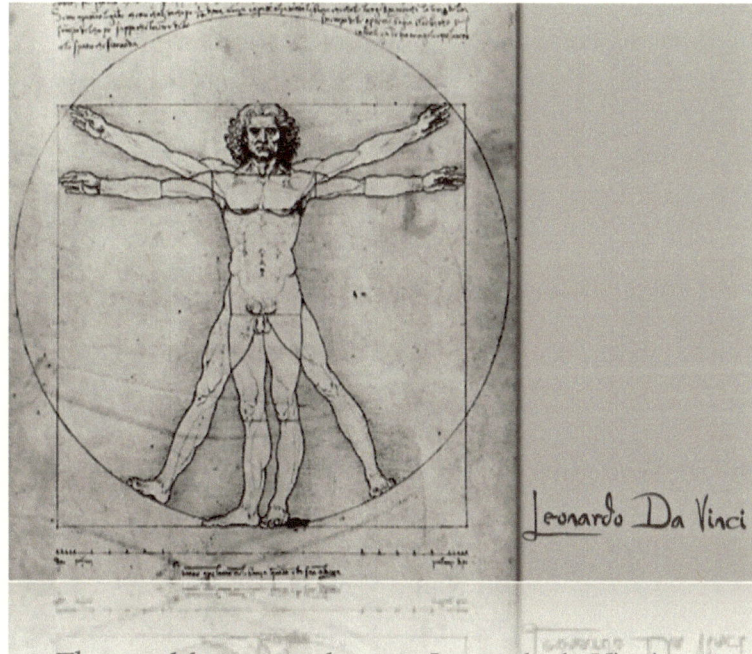

Leonardo Da Vinci

The world was used to see *Leonardo da Vinci*
(1452-1519) as a painter, not a scientist, as it used to
see Salvador Dali as a painter, and not as a poet, and
notable psychoanalyst. I questioned both these views
already at the onset of my genius research, thirty
years ago, when I found Dali's literary works and

Leonardo's scientific notebooks. Leonardo and Goethe were the avatars of a new worldview, yet during their lifetimes, their breadth of mind and holistic perception of the world was barely valued, let alone understood. Goethe's color theory was looked at with suspicion, as it was in flagrant contradiction to Newton's scientific universe.

> —Johann Wolfgang von Goethe, The Theory of Colors, New York: MIT Press, 1970, first published in 1810. See also Frederick Burwick, The Damnation of Newton: Goethe's Color Theory and Romantic Perception, New York: Walter de Gruyter, 1986, and Dennis L. Sepper, Goethe Contra Newton: Polemics and the Project of a New Science of Color, Cambridge: Cambridge University Press, 1988.

Leonardo was considered by Herman Grimm, a noted historian, in side remarks of his monograph *Life of Michelangelo*, as a flamboyant regal person, but also a bohemian and 'dark soul.'

> Lionardo is not a man that you can pass at ease, but a force that we are bound with and whose charm we cannot escape when it once has touched us. Whoever has seen Mona Lisa smile, is followed eternally by this smile, just as by Lear's fury, Macbeth's ambition, Hamlet's depression or Iphigenia's moving purity.

> —Herman Grimm, Leben Michelangelos, Wien, Leipzig: Phaidon Verlag, 1901, 42 (Translation mine)

It is as if Lionardo had within himself the need of the most daring contradictions in relation to the truly wonderful beings he was able to create. He himself, handsome, and strong as a titan, generous, surrounded with numerous servants and horses, and fantastic household, a perfect musician, charming and lovely in sight of high and low, poet, sculptor, architect, civil engineer, mechanic, a friend of counts and kings and yet as citizen of his nation a dark existence who, seldom leaving the semi-dark atmosphere of his being, finds no opportunity to invest his forces simply and freely for a great endeavor. (Id., 43-44)

Such natures, that with their extraordinary talents seem to be born only for adventure and who have kept even in the most serious and deepest endeavors of their mind a child-like playfulness, are rare, but possible appearances. Such men are of high descent; genial, beautiful, independent and glowing of yet undefined action, they walk into the world. All is open to them and in no way they encounter real, oppressive sorrow; they mold their lives that nobody than themselves understands because nobody has been born under conditions that exactly led to such a fantastic yet necessary and inescapable destiny. (Id., 44)

Grimm's picture of Leonardo lacks personal touch; it is deeply romantic and seems almost sterile. Grimm did not depict, and even less appreciate, the personal identity of the *genius* but rather painted him as a *genus*. Needless to add that in his romantic effluvia, Grimm did not lose a word on the *scientist* Leonardo, and this is all too typical for the general opinion about him before the 20th century.

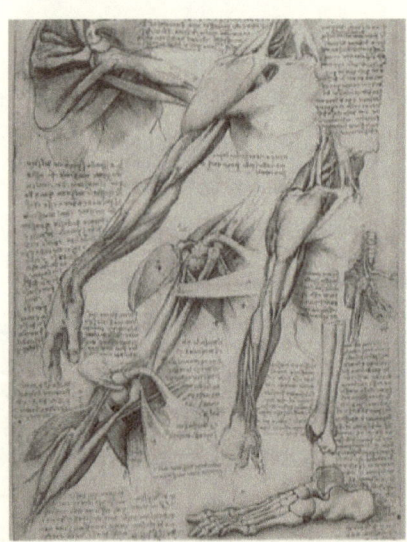

Fritjof Capra notes in his elucidating study on Leonardo, *The Science of Leonardo (2008)*, that the great polymath of the Renaissance was contrary to common belief *not a mechanistic thinker*, as were later, for example, Francis Bacon or Galileo Galilei, despite the fact that he was one of the first great inventors of modern machines, and actually very interested in machines all his life through.

—See Peter Fritz Walter, Fritjof Capra and the Systems View of Life (Great Minds Series, Vol. 3), 2015/2017.

But Leonardo did not consider the human body as a machine. Capra makes his point convincingly that modern science did not begin with Galilei, but with Leonardo, because it was Leonardo who, for the first time applied *scientific method,* logic, observation and the capacity to conceptualize a multitude of data into a single coherent and consistent theory. This was so much the more an achievement as during his lifetime science was still entangled with religion to a point that a large body of the *corpus scientia* was ecclesiastical doctrine, and as such a mix of mythic views, politically correct assumptions and a residue of observation that was for the largest part taken over from Aristotle. Capra writes:

> Leonardo da Vinci broke with this tradition. One hundred years before Galileo and Bacon, he single-handedly developed a new empirical approach to science, involving the systematic observation of nature, logical reasoning, and some mathematical formulations—the main characteristics of what is known today as the *scientific method.*

—Fritjof Capra, The Science of Leonardo: Inside the Mind of the Great Genius of the Renaissance, New York: Anchor Books, 2008, 2.

It is curious to observe that Leonardo did not formulate, at the onset of his lifelong multidisciplinary research, an intention for so doing; calling himself humbly an 'omo sanza lettere,' an uneducated man, his project was to write a manual on the 'science of painting.'

His grasp of the world was predominantly visual, so was his scientific method; it was based upon very accurate and astute observation of nature and all forms of living. Only a genius can have the abundant curiosity, the intellectual grasp and the persistence to inquire so deeply into what the eye perceives, to really get to unveil basic laws and functional connections in all living, and in all material life.

One may be baffled to see that this magnificent creator was to that point marginalized during his lifetime: none of his notebooks were published, worse, as Fritjof Capra reports, after his death, the collection of his writings and drawings, almost thirteen thousand pages, was scattered and dispersed all over Europe, stuffed in libraries, instead of having been sorted and properly published; still worse, almost half of the collection was lost. Capra writes:

> Leonardo's scientific work was virtually unknown during his lifetime and remained hidden for over two centuries after his death in 1519. His pioneering discoveries and ideas had no direct influence on the scientists who came after him, although during the subsequent 450 years his conception of a science of living forms would emerge again at various times. (…) While Leonardo's manuscripts were gathering dust in ancient European libraries, Galileo Galilei was being celebrated as the 'father of modern science.' I cannot help but argue that the true founder of modern science was Leonardo da Vinci, and I wonder how Western scientific thought would have developed had his Notebooks been known and widely studied soon after his death. (Id., 5-6)

I would like to focus for a moment on a *significant detail,* namely how Leonardo was thinking about 'life,' about living systems, and about science in relation to life. We are today familiar with the conception of life being not a linear rigid structure that is totally measurable, except when organisms have died, but a nonlinear structure of dynamic patterns, which are essentially *relationships*. Fritjof Capra has elucidated in *The Web of Life (1997)* that life is basically a structure of 'networks within networks' and that hierarchies do not exist in nature.

This view is emerging since a few decades and is called the 'systems view of life;' it is related to *deep ecology* and *systems theory* and was developed, besides Capra, mainly by Ludwig von Bertalanffy, Humberto Maturana, Francisco J. Varela, Ilya Prigogine and Ervin Laszlo. What was known from Goethe's pantheistic philosophy that considered life as an organic whole, we find it, in Capra's retrospective, equally with Leonardo. Capra writes:

> Nature as a whole was alive for Leonardo. He saw the patterns and processes in the microcosm as being similar to those in the macrocosm. (…) / While the analogy between microcosm and macrocosm goes back to Plato and was well known throughout the Middles Ages and the Renaissance, Leonardo disentangled it from its original mythical context and treated it strictly as a scientific theory. (Id., 3-4)

Capra goes as far as talking of Leonardo as 'a systemic thinker,' because of his strong synthetic thinking ability, that was able to 'interconnect observations and ideas from different disciplines.' (Id., 5)

He observes that Leonardo's visual perception was unusually sharp and accurate, and truly scientific in scope and intent, and that he also had an accurate sense of *motion*. Usually, the static eye distorts objects that are in motion. We are hardly aware of this imperfection of our sight as we today are surrounded by visual objects such as televisions, and take high-quality photographs using digital technology. But at a time when there were no photographic plates and cameras, motion was hardly ever depicted by visual artists in a realistic sense; this was simply so as most artists were unable to train their eye to a point to perceive motion correctly, and without distortion of perspective.

In addition, Capra notes, Leonardo had a view of the body that preceded quantum physics and modern spirituality. For Leonardo, 'the human body was an outward and visible expression of the soul; it was shaped by its spirit,' (Id., 11) Unlike Descartes, Leonardo never thought of the body as a machine, even though he was a brilliant engineer who designed countless machines and mechanical devices. (Id.)

Fritjof Capra notes that Leonardo had an understanding of nature that was basically *ecological* in the sense that, contrary to what Francis Bacon would advocate a century later, man was not made for dominating nature, but for *understanding nature,* and based upon that understanding, to *cooperate with nature.* From this basic worldview, Leonardo was sensible to nature's complexity and abundance, which was certainly not an attitude commonly to be found at his lifetime. In addition, he was aware of the fallacy of scientific reductionism.

> Our sciences and technologies have become increasingly narrow in their focus, and we are unable to understand our multifaceted problems from an interdisciplinary perspective. We urgently need a science that honors and respects the unity of all life, that recognizes the fundamental interdependence of

all natural phenomena, and reconnects us with the living earth. What we need today is exactly the kind of thinking and science Leonardo da Vinci anticipated and outlined five hundred years ago, at the height of the Renaissance and the dawn of modern scientific age. (Id., 12)

The genius of Leonardo is so unique because it was so versatile. It cannot be compared with anything we know today, in a culture where specialization is required and where universal genius would be frowned upon as 'generalizing and imprecise.'

Perhaps Leonardo had most in common with Aristotle, in that both men were general and precise at the same time, which is not achievable for most humans simply because of the sheer amount of data to process, ideas to develop, concepts to make, and hidden connections between seemingly separate subjects to make out and describe.

I am well aware that in stating this, I made a comparison that limps as Aristotle was certainly not a great artist, nor did he excel in inventing and conceptualizing machines of any kind. It is then the unique combination, the unique synthesis of art, science and technology that makes the genius of Leonardo.

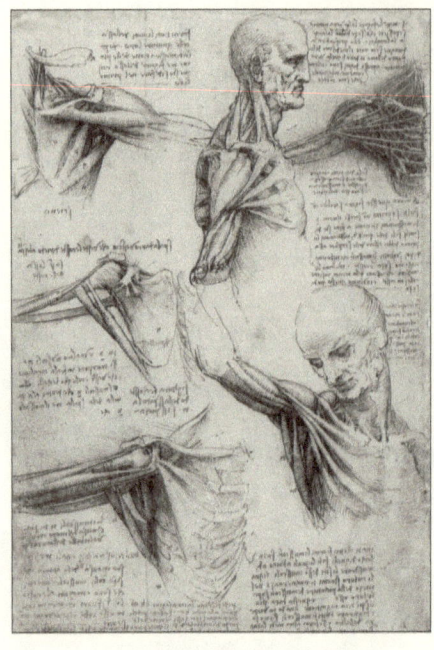

The main message of this book is that we, as a society, need to expand our understanding of the multi-faceted problems with an interdisciplinary perspective, rather than staying with the narrow focus of 'specialization' that modern science emphasizes so much. If we could see, as Leonardo did, the unity of all life, and recognize the fundamental interdependence of all natural phenomena, we would begin to design effective solutions to problems that we always thought were unsolvable.

The author's intention was thus to outline the synthesis in thinking that Leonardo achieved 500 years ago. When you consider this enormous and enormously important claim, you cannot but think this must be a tremendously timely book.

What our science achieved only recently, over the last 30 years or so, within the framework of systems theory, was for Leonardo a natural and organic way of thinking, for at the core of Leonardo's synthesis was the understanding of living forms of nature. His conception of painting was scientific, too, in that it involved for him the study of natural forms in very minute detail, in a way that to my knowledge no other artist has every undertaken. In this sense, the artist Leonardo and the scientist Leonardo cannot be separated: one part of his personality complemented the other. It is therefore important to understand both is art and his science, and then, as the author did in this book, arrive at a synthesis.

What only now emerges in modern science, namely an appreciation of the form and gestalt of matter, rather than its substance, Leonardo was lucidly aware of. He studied throughout his life the magic of water, its movements and flow nature and was by so doing a pioneer in the discipline known today as fluid dynamics. His manuscripts are filled with precise drawings of spiraling vortices.

His studies seem to not have been appreciated by previous commenters, which makes Capra's contribution in *Learning from Leonardo (2013)* a very original one, as he delivers an in-depth analysis of Leonardo's 'water science,' and he based his analysis on extensive discussions with Ugo Piomelli, professor of fluid dynamics at Queen's University in Canada.

As Leonardo observed how water and rocks interact, he undertook ground-breaking studies in geology, even to the point that he identified folds of rock strata and outlining and evolutionary perspective 300 years before Charles Darwin. Fritjof Capra also remarks in *Learning from Leonardo (2013)*

that, in addition, Leonardo made extensive inquiries about plants. While this research was first intended as studies for paintings, it became so extensive that they resulted in genuine studies about the patterns of metabolism and growth that underlie all botanical forms. Other domains of study were mechanics, known today as statics, dynamics, and kinematics, thereby inventing a great number of machines. He also compared the way humans move their body and animals, by comparison, and what fascinated him most in this field of inquiry was the flight of birds. He became almost obsessed with flying, and thus designed highly original flying machines. But his science of flight, as Capra shows with his habitual systematic approach, involved numerous sub-disciplines such as aerodynamics, human and bird anatomy, and mechanical engineering.

Capra has great merit in identifying what he calls the 'grand unifying theme' in Leonardo's explorations of both the macrocosm and the microcosm, in order to gain an understanding of the nature of life. Capra reports that this quest reached its climax in the anatomical studies he carried out in Milan and Rome when he was over sixty, especially in his investigations of the human heart. Nobody had at that time an idea how the heart functions.

Finally, when Leonardo approached old age, he became fascinated with the processes of reproduction and embryonic development.

In his embryological studies, he described the life processes of the fetus in the womb in great detail.

Chapter Two

The Genius of Wilhelm Reich

Introduction

It is rather strange to realize that over the entire course of our scientific history, those who were the real scientists were taken as freaks, and blamed and plagued to be charlatans, quacks, make-believes, moonwalkers, daydreamers or paranoid doctors, while half-baked mediocre and dry academics without the juice of genius were given laurels and Nobel prizes.

This was so from the Middle Ages to modern times and from Paracelsus to Nikola Tesla, invariably so.

In our postmodern era of political and social rebellion against a big brother state that is going to be more and more cannibalizing our children, we seem to find it almost normal that those who do things officially are the mafia, and those who are thought to be mafia are the real doers.

We seem to take it for granted that large-scale *perversion* has set in somewhere around the times of Hammurabi, which resulted in things, people and institutions being upside-down.

One result of this sad history is that young people have largely lost their trust in our governments and are focused upon conspiracies. It seems to me that conspiracy thinking has replaced what formerly was called a 'critical mind.' I myself have still received an education that, not because it was called *humanistic,* was value-based, one of these values being *social criticism*. However, conspiracy thinking is not critical, it is *pseudo-critical and counter-ideological*, and this is not surprising as humanistic education has almost completely disappeared and was replaced by standard education.

To become a critical thinker, one needs to be a *scientific thinker* first. Without correct reasoning, criticism is dull and superficial, and can never be convincing. It may even come over as assault, while criticism naturally is a positive contribution and as such constructive. In conspiracy thinking the real penetration of the matter at stake is missing, as it is largely replaced by *speculation*.

To put it as a slogan, we could say that science is intellectual penetration, while conspiracy science is *political science fiction*, and can easily lead to absolutist and fascist attitudes and opinions.

And here I must alert the reader: speculation is not intuition; it has nothing to do with the gift of genius that anticipates paradigmatic changes. Speculation comes from a certain overdrive of thinking, while intuition is like a lighting between thoughts. In all great scientific novelty, there is intuition.

In other words, speculation leads to circular thought, while intuition leads to novelty in the form of *new thought*.

Einstein intuited relativity theory in a dream prior to its formulation as a scientific revolution. His mind was able to perceive the truth of 'relativity' in a holistic vision prior to the logical, critical, and methodological drafting of the theory in its scientific terms and vocabulary.

In scientific genius, there is *intuition*, not speculation. The science fiction author speculates, but the science author *intuits*, and here we are facing two worlds that are quite apart. The first world is popular gimmick that takes the approximation as exact truth, the second world is scientific isolation that suffers from the fact that unscientific minds *take methodology spiced with intuitive insight as approximation*. By the same token, the first world is where the mass mind and our popular science magazines are thriving, the second world is the ivory tower of our science gurus and saints who, while being meticulously methodic, know that in a quantum world, the idea of scientific objectivity is a myth.

When Wilhelm Reich published his works on orgasmic sanity and the prevention of sexual pathology through the means of a truthful education, he was suspected to be a paranoid quack, and was defamed and persecuted over the main part of his scientific career, to end his life in jail.

What is more, the vulgarization of science through the mass media has added another pitfall, which is to classify scientific achievement not according to the *scientific novelty* it brings, but according to its popularity among those who, for the most part, don't even know what they are talking about. This is really what is called 'giving pearls to the pigs.' Confronting the scientist with the mass mind is doing injustice to science and injury to the scientist, in the name of the sanctified stupidity of the masses.

Our fanatical obsession with democracy is misplaced where it exposes the novelty bringer to the scribes and pharisaics, the 'established' and the common hypocrite as the prototype of Judas in modern times. This will not make science any better, while it certainly makes those richer who are eternally second-guessing life. In the contrary, we have to ask for more protection of scientific genius, and our governments should provide a safe haven for scientific novelty that may well shock old virgins, neurotic churchgoers and the common lot of *homo normalis*.

We give that space for creative delirium to the artist, why do we deny it to the scientist? We allow artists to live in a certain protected cavern, surrounded by friends and donors, art benefactors and soft-minded agents, but we expose our best scientists to the tiger-claws of our ferocious populace, just like in the Roman games.

What is it that makes the masses resent the science genius while they do not really bother about perversities artistic geniuses may indulge in?

The suspicion, the estrangement and the hatred that the revolutionary scientist faces comes from the fact that he anticipates social change, and often helps triggering it, while the artist who lives against social and legal rules just satisfies a personal need for space and freedom.

Society eternally fears change because it confronts established conventions previously thought to be set in stone and undisputed. Social change is likely to happen for we are living in the field of all possibilities.

Reich had a *profound vision* for society and like visionaries before him, he was persecuted.

Jesus of Nazareth was legally executed not because he indulged in certain personal fancies, but because he was showing a viable way of living that was in accordance with *love*, not with *law* alone, thereby subtly suggesting that love is superior to law, or that all law has to be interpreted in a spirit of love.

That his vision was right and sound, we know it all today, while at his lifetime the very idea of love being superior to law was revolutionary!

When we read through the biographies and autobiographies of outstanding scientists, we see that they all had and have a *social vision*, that they can see and imagine how their scientific novelty will affect social togetherness, society, and the way people live and behave in time and space.

I found this especially true for Wilhelm Reich who was building a long-needed bridge over the gap between natural science and social sciences.

> —Fritjof Capra, in several of his books, especially in The Turning Point (1987), writes eloquently about Reich and his achievements, and he especially notes this point, and acknowledges the pioneering role that Reich played for our modern understanding of science and social sciences being two parts of one functional whole.

Because of his social vision, Reich was then able to see the functional link between the repression of our natural emotions and fascism as a social disease.

As emotional stuckness and neurosis typically go along with the person's *denial of complexity*, so do fascist regimes belittle and deny life's intrinsic patterned complexity and come up with simplistic single-causative formulae for solving social and political problems.

For today's scientific elite, this link cannot be unthought, but for generations before Reich, there was simply no connection to be seen between the two phenomena.

Another element present in the life stories of revolutionary scientists is their deep concern for being *benefactors to society,* their care for bringing about positive changes for each one of us, which is often frowned upon as 'misplaced enthusiasm' or *idealism.*

Really, the painful paradox is that their zeal to bring good to the masses lets those masses reject them, and meet them with afterthoughts and suspicion; it's the tragic element of *purity meeting an impure mind,* or sainthood meeting vulgarity. This was affecting me personally on an emotional level when I was reading those life stories, and I was reading them over years and years as my favorite pastime.

As a matter of analogy, then, the study of science cannot be separated from the study of the people who do science, the *scientists.*

This leads to more coherence, as scientific novelty cannot be really understood without understanding the one who brought it about. When I contemplate the entire life path of a scientist, I can more soundly and *holistically* understand how he or she came to make the discoveries they made. Then, I can exclude or forebear an element of randomness as a pitfall in non-scientific thinking.

There simply is no randomness in intelligent people's professional lives, but the mass mind suspects it to be present in order to veil their ignorance of certain facts or *relationships between things* that seem to be unrelated at first sight.

Let me again provide an example from the turbulent and dramatic life story of Wilhelm Reich. When Reich was completing his orgasm research, and before he formulated his theory of orgonotic health, there was an episode that often is described by biographers as a sort of *intermezzo*, and the deep connection is regularly overlooked between Reich's orgasm research and his discovery of the orgonotic streaming in the subtle energy body. This interlude, as it were, is Reich's experiment with what later was called the *Sapa Bions*.

The event bears an element of randomness, and Reich's detractors always played on lacking connectivity between Reich's discoveries as a matter of proving him wrong or paranoid where he was simply lucid. When Reich discovered that desert sand, when burnt and put in distilled water, was irradiating a blue-green aura that vitalizes plants, animals and the human body, he discovered that what he found to be *sexual energy* in his orgasm research is actually a manifestation of the cosmic energy or *life force*, which cycles through both living and inanimate substance. The sunlight filled the sand particles with that force and through burning those particles and thereby melting them, the energy was freed and irradiated in the form of *orgonotic radiation* or streaming. When we look at the bion

experiment as an *isolated event*, it certainly bears an element of randomness, but that is because our observer perspective is *reductionist* and not holistic.

For me it is obvious that destiny helped Reich to find the truth through the cosmic play of *synchronicity*, and on this very line of reasoning, the bion experiments are to be seen as synchronistic events that led to a further sprocket in the chain of causality in Reich's scientific life and in his research on the cosmic life energy.

From the Hero to the Human

My reaction to Reich's research went through a certain pattern; in other words, it was a journey, starting back in 1975. I just read all I could get, then learnt about his fate and death in jail, then went through a revolt and joined the rings of the 'Reichians' in Berlin, the hagiographers, the groupings, then wrote an essay about his research. Then only was I able to eventually understand Reich as the person he really was: the scientist, the doctor, the discoverer.

It was a convoluted journey through thesis, antithesis and synthesis for gaining a *somewhat accurate* image about Reich that was backed by facts, not by myths. I should say that contrary to those who write pamphlets about Reich, I really have studied his works, not just some of them, but the *integrality of his published and non-published writings, including translations.*

Myron Sharaf, author of a famed biography of Wilhelm Reich, said in a lecture on *Orgonotic Functionalism* in Berlin that Reich was always to him like great music.

> The wonderful thing about Reich, it's like great music. If you haven't heard great music in a few months, it sounds like you never heard it before. And when you read Reich after not having read him for awhile, it feels like you haven't read him before.

—Myron Sharaf, Orgonotic Functionalism, Lecture in Berlin, Germany, 22 October 1989, published in: Heretic's Notebook, ed. by James DeMeo (2002), 45-54, at 45. See also Myron Sharaf, Fury on Earth: A Biography of Wilhelm Reich (1983).

As uncanny and potentially unscientific as this statement sounds, it is true. I read Reich upon enrolling in law school in Germany, and I am still today reading Reich, forty years later. Every time I read him, it's as if reading him for the first time—why? Because his diction is so immediate and his scientific truth so shining and authentic that you feel reading him for the first time in your life. And every time it's a transforming and deeply enlightening experience!

As a research lawyer, I have studied the circumstances of Reich's imprisonment, the whole discussion he, and his lawyer, had with the authorities. The complete information was only recently released and the declassified FBI record published.

—Federal Bureau of Investigation, Dr. Wilhelm Reich, BUFILE: 100-14601, PDF, 813 pages.

This extensive dossier contains all the letters he wrote to the authorities and to his defense attorney. The letters he wrote to the authorities, especially to FBI Director John Edgar Hoover, bore a perhaps deliberately offensive tone: the language was rude and coarse, and some of the allegations seemed absurd. There was a tendency throughout to dramatize matters, and to blow the emotional whistle. In fact, the situation was not as dramatic. There was a simple violation of an FDA injunction by shipping one of his accumulators interstate to a client.

The FDA had disapproved the orgone accumulator because of lacking or contradictory evidence of its healing powers. In such a situation, a wise person would not fight but try to conciliate, get out of trouble, and then work for a later approval of his medical device by the FDA.

Reich did the contrary, he not only defied the court action by not entering an appearance with the argument that the whole procedure was based upon 'fraud,' then, arrested, continued to tell the authorities they were 'pranking gangsters' and 'psychopathic murderers,' participating in a huge conspiracy that was intending to 'destroy mankind.'

Honestly, one wouldn't think that a serious researcher, facing contradiction, would act out in such a way; his reaction could only corroborate negative rumors about him, and give his enemies right in their assumptions—if those assumptions were true or not is not even the question in such a case. And as a side remark, I may be allowed to add here that either his lawyer was incompetent or Reich overruled his advice by submitting documents to the authorities without prior approval by his legal counsel.

In addition, he was proclaiming himself throughout this trial as 'the discoverer of the cosmic life energy.' He even signed his official trial correspondence with the title 'Counsel for the Discovery of the Cosmic Life Energy.'

I have demonstrated with my own long-term research that Reich was certainly *not* the discoverer of the human energy field, while he made an important contribution in a legacy of major scientific novelty that dozens of scientists from around the world were working on since times immemorial.

The *Wilhelm Reich Trust* in Rangeley, Maine, now reveal on their website an unpublished statement by Reich, that gives an answer, without however mentioning with one word the trial correspondence:

> I am well aware of the fact that the human race has known about the existence of a universal energy related to life for many ages. However, the basic task of natural science consisted of making this energy usable. This is the sole difference between my work and all preceding knowledge.

The answer is that Reich was *emotionally entangled* with his work, to a point to perceive adverse reactions to his research as targeting his person. While it is documented that Reich was a walking tempest, known for his 'explosions' of rage, he could not forgive others any intellectual mediocrity, or the slightest lack of understanding of his daringly novel research topics. When facing a discussion, he would not quietly explain matters from the perspective of his research, but become absolute and personal in his responses, thereby transforming people who were merely critical or skeptical into lifelong enemies.

Interestingly, and symptomatically so, I have been in touch with people who were close to Reich, and who work on the lines of his research, such as Mary Boyd Higgins, trustee of his foundation and curator of the Wilhelm Reich Trust in Rangeley, Maine, and others, and was wondering about their *categorical, unfriendly and aggressive tone,* while I was doing non-funded research work on Reich to write an essay on his merits as a maverick researcher on the human energy field.

The Genius Defined by His Work

I will now shortly explain why and how Reich was a true scientific genius—while as a simple human, he was certainly not up to the same standard of excellence!

However, it is important to remember that research on the life force, the *secret of life,* was considered heresy under the Church's definition of science. That is why great scientists like Paracelsus, Swedenborg, or Mesmer who knew about the ether and observed the moving and alternating current of our emotional body had a hard time to survive times of utter darkness and superstition. Paracelsus had to appear before the ecclesiastical court several times in his life for defending his miraculous healing successes against the Inquisition's allegation he had used witchcraft to bring them about. At that time, according to the Church's doctrine only recognized saints were allowed to do miracles, while the Inquisition in all other cases generally subsumed miracles and healing miracles under the witchcraft definition contained in *The Malleus Maleficarum (The Witch Hammer)*, first published in 1486.

Franz Anton Mesmer equally was slandered and persecuted, once famous, for his research on what he called *animal magnetism*. And yet these men seem to have discovered something for the West which was never disputed in the East, that is, a bioplasmatic energy as a functional catalyzer of life in that it penetrates all, animates all, fills all, vitalizes all and destroys all again when a natural life cycle is at its end.

The Chinese speak of *ch'i*, the Japanese of *ki*, the Germans of *Lebensenergie* or *Vitalkraft*, the French of *élan vital* or *force nerveuse*, Anglo-Saxons of *bioenergy* or the *human energy field*, the Indians of *kundalini* or *prana* and most tribal peoples of *mana* or *wakonda*.

Also the old Egyptians knew the vital energy. We can suppose that their notion of *ka*, a term often to be found in Pharaonic hieroglyphs denotes that same universal energy.

Among tribal populations, the Kahunas from Hawaii, within their *Huna* religion, have extensively and systematically studied the *life force* that they call *mana*. This teaching about *mana*, the vital force, and *aka*, a protruding bioplasmatic substance that is known as *ectoplasm*, forms an integral part of their religion that, for this reason, may be called a scientific religion.

—See, for example, Max Freedom Long, The Secret Science at Work: The Huna Method as a Way of Life, Marina del Rey: De Vorss Publications, 1995, originally published in 1953, and Growing Into Light: A Personal Guide to Practicing the Huna Method, Marina del Rey: De Vorss Publications, 1955, as well as Erika Nau, Self-Awareness Through Huna, Virginia Beach: Donning, 1981.

It is obvious that these different views of the same thing have brought about divergent scientific experiments that in turn resulted in contradictory scientific results. As we have to account for the observer bias, we have to look into the *paradigmatic assumptions* these science traditions make prior to observing nature. The Chinese or Japanese scientist sees life through *dynamic-energetic* glasses, while the Western scientist observes living processes through *static-materialistic* glasses.

This is how Western science could get at the point to deny the existence of the *vital energy*, that is by vehemently blinding out the existence of the *ether*. It is a fact of science history that still Albert Einstein joined in this blindfolding tradition, but probably under false premises.

—James DeMeo, Dayton Miller's Ether-Drift Experiments: A Fresh Look, in: James DeMeo (Ed.), Heretic's Notebook: Emotions, Ether-Drift and Cosmic Life Energy, Pulse of the Planet, Issue 5 (Spring 2002), Oregon: Orgone Biophysical Research Laboratory, Inc., 2002, 114-130.

Only recently, the cutting-edge forefront of science under the pulpit of widely respected integral thinkers such as Ervin Laszlo, William Tiller or Ken Wilber now holds as true the perennial intuition that there is *no vacuum but actually a plenum,* filled namely with a creative space *which assumes vital biogenic functions.* Now, this alternative branch in modern science clearly sees that the quantum field, unified field or quantum vacuum is the root cause of all possible field phenomena, especially for what in quantum physics is called the *zero-point field,* and what Laszlo has called *A-field.*

—Ervin Laszlo, Science and the Akashic Field: An Integral Theory
of Everything, Rochester: Inner Traditions, 2004 and Ken Wilber,
Sex, Ecology, Spirituality: The Spirit of Evolution, Boston:
Shambhala, 2000.

Presently we grow into a *global consciousness* while
in more and more isolated areas countless
complications accumulate, because we have neglected
holistic thinking and continue to apply local solutions
to global challenges.

Now almost everybody talks about global
solutions, but at Reich's lifetime, this was a rare
exception. Reich was a pioneer in holistic, or
ecological, science, at a time where holistic
consciousness was a no brainer for the majority of
scientists. Furthermore, Reich can be seen as a
mediator between East and West. His discovery and
scientific corroboration of the cosmic energy or
bioenergy, that he called *orgone*, is in full alignment
with the Eastern knowledge tradition. He was fully
aware of the historical background of his research. He
knew about *ch'i* and what in India is called *prana*; he
also knew about the alchemists and Anton Mesmer's
revolutionary research. There is a compilation of
historical sources done by Reich's assistant, which is
available at the Wilhelm Reich Trust.

—Arthur Hahn, A Review of the Theories, Dating from the 17th Century, on the Origins of Life, Maine: Orgone Institute Press (without publishing date).

In fact, besides ancient China and India, this knowledge was part of perennial science and shared by scholars in old Babylon, Egypt, Crete and later Paracelsus in Switzerland. Reich, it is true, did not quote from these sources since he had grown in a natural science tradition that considered such sources only randomly as scientific, and primarily as *philosophical*.

From the perspective of *perennial science*, this is actually the right expression because philosophy was from Antiquity considered to be the queen of all sciences; it also encompassed natural science, which today assumes an unruly supremacy over the other sciences.

In fact, psychic research is also dealing with natural phenomena and there is no reason to exclude them from natural science! The original concept of philosophy in antiquity encompassed also astrology, numerology, magic and all other 'hermetic' sciences. The ancient scientist was a holistically oriented researcher, and not a fragmented specialist.

Reich's *orgone accumulator* was preceded by
Mesmer's magnetic healing techniques which are
based on exactly the same principle. Producing rain
through bioenergetic projection is known to Tibetan
lamas and native shamans since times immemorial.
UFO's that Reich was concerned with at the end of his
life are a fact for most psychic researchers today. The
terra lines that Reich found as energy pipelines of the
earth were known to Druid sages, thousands of years
ago. Stonehenge is built on a crossroads of those lines,
a place which accumulates and magnifies earth
radiation and at the same time produces the UFO
phenomenon.

Perhaps without having been aware of it, Reich
came closer to the research of *parapsychologists and
spiritual healers* than to what traditionally is
considered as medical science. It was perhaps his

tragedy to have sought time and again the approval of his doctor colleagues rather than addressing his revolutionary research primarily to the common sense of a select audience of lay persons, and perhaps in collaboration with psychics, clairvoyants and aura healers.

But here, he was probably not broad-minded enough, or trapped in the myth of 'exact science' as an evolutionary improvement over what was considered as 'primitive science,' without considering that those latter sciences actually form part of the perennial science tradition, and thus have been time-tested over the course of human scientific history. Not to talk about the *scientific view of shamanism* of which Reich never seemed to have an idea, but that is these days acknowledged as a truly scientific alternative worldview that observes nature in exactly the assiduous and meticulous way as any Eastern or Western scientist, and that derives very clear and practically applicable solutions from this observation, for example for healing and for handling human emotions.

To this day, the real understanding of Reich's genius is not coming from the side of medical doctors but from disciplines such as holistic and spiritual healers, bioenergy healers, body-workers, Reiki specialists, parapsychologists, mediums and spiritual gurus. Reich was perhaps too much concerned with his reputation as a natural scientist, medical doctor and psychoanalyst instead of taking a broader viewpoint and addressing his speech to those who are able to listen.

A Scientific Genius

After the foregoing elucidations, we may ask what specifically it is that brings Reich's scientific genius on a line with Leonardo's and Einstein's, or negatively put, what it is that ordinary scientists lack out on? This approach may sound a bit elitist but it is only through comparison that we can elucidate what *genius* is because it is not something remote of the human condition, but somehow a *higher octave* of it. In other words, geniuses, in whatever field they operate, also only 'cook with water,' but theirs is a better soup than instant Knorr.

I have not known Reich in person, so all my conclusions are based solely on his literary production. On the other hand, this is not necessarily a handicap, precisely for the reasons I advanced above.

Many of Reich's contemporaries have misjudged Reich not because they have known him in person, but because they have *not* known his books. He voiced it very clearly several times in the letter exchange with Alexander S. Neill, saying that those who are the most negative about him have never met him in person, nor read any of his books. In fact, most of them were simply falling in line with the rumors about 'the sex-obsessed quack.'

> — Wilhelm Reich, Alexander S. Neill, Record of a Friendship: The Correspondence of Wilhelm Reich and A. S. Neill, New York, Farrar, Straus & Giroux, 1981.

It is for these reasons probably the best approach to render conclusions about the researcher exclusively on the basis of his research; and there are some additional reasons. Reich was not only a genius in the way he did scientific research and came to conclusive insights; he also was a genius in how he was able to communicate the whole process of his investigations comprehensively to even a lay reader, and how he presented the high amount of data, in their complexity, in his books. It is because of Reich's scientific honesty combined with his pedagogical talent that we are able today to retrace his *scientific methodology* solely on the basis of his books.

I have shown in my review of some of the lesser known books by Dr. Reich that his underlying science concept had firmly embodied the *Gestalt*. Reich's genius as a scientist was his gift of observation, and his talent to see not single elements of a process, but the *whole of the process*. Reich was here really different from the mainstream bunch of his professional colleagues; did he live today, he would probably be considered as one of our leading-edge scientists. Generally speaking, when we observe living processes, we can either put our focus on single elements, or the *substance*, or we can focus on the *process*, and the *form*. Both form and substance are present in living systems.

Our culture has created the line as a symbol for evolution. However, the line is an artificial construct, inexistent in nature, a purely mental, mathematical, achievement.

Evolution is cyclic. It allows the line only in combination with the circle, so as to say, resulting in the spiral.

Merriam-Webster's Dictionary defines the spiral as 'relating to the advancement to higher levels through a series of cyclical movements.' The curving movement of the spiral is what it has in common with the circle; the increase or decrease in size of the spiral is a function of its moving upward or downward.

The spiral is by far the dominating form to be found in nature, and in all natural processes. It is a symbol for *evolution* in general. Life is coded in the spiraled double-helix of the DNA molecule. The spiral is the expression of the periodic, systemic and cyclic development that is in accordance with the laws of life.

The progression of the spiral shows that it *always carries its root,* however transporting it through every cycle onto a higher level or dimension; whereas the line leaves its root forever. All towers of Babel are manifestations of the line: they are linear and are created by linear thought.

True growth is always cyclic and spiraled, and nonlinear. While in our days, as a result of the insights of quantum physics, molecular biology and psychoneuroimmunology, we have a glimpse of these truths, this was certainly not the case at Reich's lifetime. Most of his enemies were those linear-thinking, reductionist scientists who were raised in a tradition that did not allow the third option *(tertium non datur)*, which means they were following a strictly causal logic, in alignment with Aristotelian and later ecclesiastical tradition. One needed to be a genius, at that time, to break through these limitations, which are, as Krishnamurti showed with convincing power, *limitations of thought*, and not epistemological flaws. One needed to be a systemic thinker, a holistic thinker, to keep true to *intuitive logic*, even in cases where conventional logic delivered no or contradictory results.

On the subject of bringing in *Gestalt* thinking in the logic of healing, Manly P. Hall, in his book *The Secret Teachings of All Ages (1928/2003)*, writes about Paracelsus:

> Paracelsus discovered that in many cases plants revealed by their shape the particular organs of the human body which they served most effectively. The medical system of Paracelsus was based on the theory that by removing the diseased etheric mumia from the organism of the patient and causing it to be accepted into the nature of some distant and disinterested thing of comparatively little value, it was possible to divert from the patient the flow of the archaeus which had been continually revitalizing and nourishing the malady. Its vehicle of expression being transplanted, the archaeus necessarily accompanied its mumia, and the patient recovered. (Id., 347)

It was *Gestalt* considerations and the insight that nature is basically formed from *patterns* and not from randomly arranged matter that led to researchers recently corroborating the age-old idea that our universe is *holographic,* and thus programmed in *dynamic patterns* that are all mutually interconnected. Ervin Laszlo writes in *Science and the Akashic Field (2004):*

> In a holographic recording—created by the interference pattern of two light beams—there is no one-to-one correspondence between points on the surface of the object that is recorded and points in the recording itself. Holograms carry information in a distributed form, so all the information that makes up a hologram is present in every part of it. The points that make up the recording of the object's surface are present throughout the interference patterns recorded on the photographic plate: in a way, the image of the object is enfolded throughout the plate. As a result, when any small piece of the plate is illuminated, the full image of the object appears, though it may be fuzzier than the image resulting from illuminating the entire plate. (Id., 55)

It is certainly true what Emerson wrote in his essay *Self-Reliance,* that 'all history resolves itself very easily into the biography of a few stout and earnest persons.' Reich was one of them, whatever one may think about him as a private person, as a feeling-failing human.

Some of the insights Reich developed over the course of his life as a physician, psychoanalyst and bioenergy researcher, mainly in his book on the prevention of sexual pathology, *Children of the Future (1950/1983)*, are highly important still in our days.

The solutions to these complex problems cannot come as a fortunate strike of heaven, but will, if ever, be the result of careful analysis and cross-disciplinary synthesis of research results across national borders, and through an effort of international or supranational cooperation.

The Nature of Orgone

Naturally, the first question to ask at the starting point of this paragraph is: 'What kind of energy is orgone, and what is it exactly that Reich discovered or rediscovered?'

More precisely, let us ask if orgone energy is a form of electricity or bioelectricity, or perhaps a variant of electromagnetic fields?

Reich asked this question several times over the course of his scientific life and each and every time his formulation of the question became more accurate. This was, at the same time, how Reich developed his scientific terminology to describe what he had observed. While before the discovery of the orgone, Reich still spoke of bioelectricity, after the formulation of *orgonomy*, he expressly revoked his earlier terminology, stressing that while orgone energy is bringing about electric and thermic phenomena, it is *not identical with these phenomena.*

> —Wilhelm Reich, The Bioelectrical Investigation of Sexuality and Anxiety (1935). I owe this insight to Bernd Senf, author and bioenergy researcher in Berlin, Germany, and Mary Boyd Higgins, Director of the Wilhelm Reich Trust and Trustee of the Wilhelm Reich Infant Trust, Rangeley, Maine, USA.

After the insights gained through Reich's pioneering work and the opening of consciousness triggered by his bioenergy research, one may begin to understand why the mainstream of modern physics is so concerned about keeping up the old order.

Quantum physics is busy with its particle accelerators that eat up funding resources by the millions of dollars every day, without any significant and tangible results, and *without reflecting about how to integrate orgone research constructively in the existing mathematic model of reality;* in fact the present model could be creatively transformed so as to fit the existence of a larger vibrational and energy-fueled reality that is by and large to replace, in the long run, the materialistic and mechanistic model of observing nature.

Despite the cutting-edge research that now emerges with holistic and integral thinkers such as Bohm, Capra, Laszlo, Sheldrake, Talbot, or Wilber, Western science in its totality seems to cling to a reality model that blinds out the existence of a cosmic information field as the basic creator mold.

Fritjof Capra, as a rare authority figure, expressly recognized the validity and high impact of Reich's orgone research in his book *The Turning Point (1982/1987):*

> From the very beginning of his medical research, Reich was keenly interested in the role of energy in the functioning of living organisms, and one of the main goals of his psychoanalytic work was to associate the sexual drive, or libido, which Freud saw as an abstract psychological force, with concrete energy flowing through the physical organism. This approach led Reich to the concept of bioenergy, a fundamental form of energy that permeates and governs the entire organism and manifests itself in

the emotions as well as in the flow of bodily fluids and other biophysical movements. Bioenergy, according to Reich, flows in wave movements and its basic dynamic characteristic is pulsation. (Id., 377)

However, earlier on in the same book, he writes that despite the merits of orgone research, the recognition of the ether was a scientific error, 'as already Albert Einstein had proven.'

> One of the nineteenth-century developments was the discovery and investigation of electric and magnetic phenomena that involved a new type of force and could not be described appropriately by the mechanistic model. The important step was taken by Michael Faraday and completed by Clerk Maxwell— the first one of the great experimenters in the history of science, the second a brilliant theorist. Faraday and Maxwell not only studied the effects of the electric and magnetic forces, but made the forces themselves the primary object of their investigation. (…) This theory, called electrodynamics, culminated in the realization that light was in fact a rapidly alternating electromagnetic field traveling through space in the form of waves. In spite of these far-reading changes, Newtonian mechanics still held its position as the basis of all physics. Maxwell himself tried to explain his results in mechanical terms, interpreting the fields as states of mechanical stress in a very light, all-pervasive medium called ether, and the

electromagnetic waves as elastic waves of this ether. However, he used several mechanical interpretations of his theory at the same time and apparently took none of them really seriously, knowing intuitively that the fundamental entities in his theory were the fields and not the mechanical models. It remained for Einstein to clearly recognize this fact in our century, when he declared that no ether existed, and that the electromagnetic fields were physical entities in their own right which could travel through empty space and could not be explained mechanically. (Id., 57)

The Einstein Affair

After inquiring into the true, and not the falsely admitted results of the *Michelson-Morley experiment,* I do not see evidence for Capra's point.

Apart from the controversy about this experiment that conditioned Einstein's later position regarding the ether, I contend that Einstein *did not refute the existence of the ether,* and this from a purely logical point of view. That Einstein did not acknowledge the existence of the ether is without a doubt, but from a point of science methodology, there is well *a difference between a scientist not acknowledging* a certain observation or theory and a scientist *explicitly disproving* the observation or theory. The latter, at least after what has been published and discussed about the matter, has not been effected by Einstein.

Besides there is an open controversy that was the subject matter of the so-called *Reich-Einstein Affair*, and that is not solved until this day. In this documented scientific correspondence between Wilhelm Reich and Albert Einstein, the point of discussion was an astounding temperature difference at the upper end of the orgone accumulator that contradicted the *Second Law of Thermodynamics*, the so-called *Law of Entropy*. The website of the *Wilhelm Reich Infant Trust* explains:

> On December 30, 1940, Reich wrote a letter to Albert Einstein asking to meet with him to discuss a difficult and urgent scientific matter, the discovery of a specific biologically effective energy which in many ways behaves differently from anything that is known about electromagnetic energy. They met soon afterward and this documentary volume makes available their subsequent correspondence, particularly as it related to the temperature difference experiment with the orgone energy accumulator.
>
> —The correspondence is documented as The Einstein Affair: History of the Discovery of the Life Energy, Documentary Volume A-XI-E Wilhelm Reich, Biographical Material, Orgone Institute Press, 1953.

This source actually suffices to declare Capra's point of view as irrelevant, for when we talk about orgone energy, we are, according to Reich, *not dealing with electromagnetic fields.*

While Einstein initially was puzzled when effectively noting the temperature difference at the upper end of the accumulator that clearly was in contradiction with the law of entropy, he eventually forwarded 'methodological objections' against the setup of the experiment. Reich replied in detail to Einstein's objections, which the latter only met with silence. As Einstein was involved in other controversies, and has brushed off other scientific exchanges in similar ways, to remember only his reply to Heisenberg on the subject of quantum physics' *Uncertainty Principle*, reported as *God Does Not Play Dice*, there is a high probability that Reich's position is true here as to the historical and scientific facts.

Reich's Pioneering Work

REFERENCES

Let me first mention some erudite studies that explain in comprehensive terms Reich's sometimes difficult-to-grasp insights and discoveries. From an abundance of literature in English language that is available in the meantime, I made a clear choice and gave the preference to Myron Sharaf, *Fury on Earth: A Biography of Wilhelm Reich (1994)* and Ola Raknes, *Wilhelm Reich and Orgonomy (1970/1971)*.

ESSENTIAL DISCOVERIES

What were the essential discoveries Reich made regarding *orgonomy* and *sex economy?* How did he get to those findings?

Reich first completed his diploma as a medical doctor and then developed a keen interest for psychoanalysis. He became one of the most brilliant students of Sigmund Freud, but their relationship soon ended in contradiction and estrangement because of Reich's engagement for the cause of the sexual liberation of the child. In fact, Reich was less interested in psychology as he was in sexological research and consulting; his basic approach to therapy was focused upon *healing the split of the psychosomatic unity* that he recognized in the etiology of all functional diseases.

As a result of his therapeutic methodology, Dr. Reich found that, logically, in all functional diseases there is also a *more or less profound disturbance* in the natural and harmonious balance of the bioenergy.

Twenty years before Masters & Johnson's sex research, Reich inquired into the function of the sexual climax, and found that all his neurosis patients, without exception, suffered from sexual dysfunctions and a more or less heavy inhibition to reach the full climax during orgasm.

Thus, a direct causal link was established, for the first time in modern sex research, between psychic or mental illness, on one hand, and sexual disturbances, on the other.

Freud theoretically knew about this link and many of his writings show that he was even acutely aware of it. But the body taboo in psychoanalysis excluded the therapist's direct interference with the body of the patient.

Reich boldly broke with this taboo and put hands on!

This estranged him from his colleagues and even from psychoanalysis as a whole, and as a consequence, he was ostracized and excluded from the International Psychoanalytic Association.

—What Reich touched in his patients were their armored bodies, hardened muscles and distorted postures whereas in classical psychoanalysis the patient's body was taboo for the therapist and not even within sight of the doctor during the sessions (the classical position requiring that there be no touch and no eye contact between patient and psychoanalyst).

However, for Reich this was the decisive new turn that prepared his move into what today still is considered as the classical Reichian bodywork. This form of therapy, as opposed to psychoanalysis, is a purely body-centered psychosomatic approach that heals neurosis from inside out, gradually dissolving the somatic armor while working toward vulnerability.

Thus the patient is sensitized and guided back toward his or her full capacity to feeling and giving.

Reich quickly went beyond, publishing about the social implications of his sex research, and thus describing the larger picture of his insights in the bioenergetic functionality of the human organism. In fact, he was the only one at his time to comprehend the gravity of the collective sickness of what later was going to be called 'the sick society.'

—Krishnamurti once said: 'It is no measure of health to be well adjusted to a profoundly sick society.'

From there to his leading research about the nature of fascism was but one step. Freud who was alarmed about Reich's new research endeavors, is known to have replied in a heated discussion with Reich:

—Culture has to prevail!

Reich did not agree. He could not see any value in preserving an insane culture that was based upon a distorted value system that creates schizoid and paranoid humans.

From about this time, Reich was put in one pot with the *Kulturfeinde*, and with communists.

—Reich was for a certain time active member of the KPD, the German Communist Party.

The public discussion of his research and also his person became increasingly heated, irrational and aggressive.

Reich's greatest merit is perhaps his discovery of the universal *principle of sex economy* that reflects a basic organizational structure in which all living is coded.

Furthermore, Reich forged this principle as a sociopolitical imperative for the reintegration of sexuality in a future healthy society that he envisioned. One of the most important ingredients of sex economy is the *principle of self-regulation* that he discovered by simply observing natural growth processes.

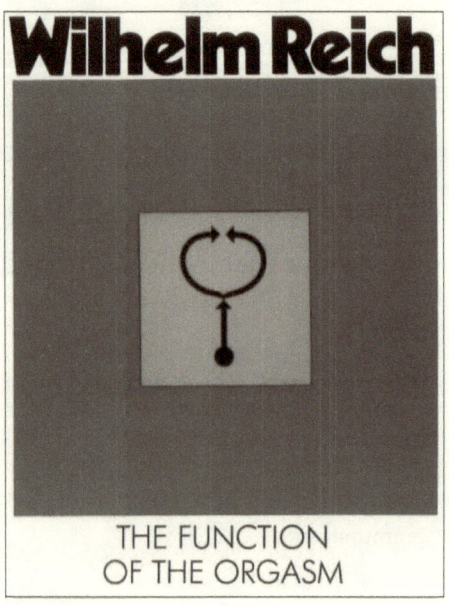

Wilhelm Reich

THE FUNCTION
OF THE ORGASM

Nature, unlike human society, is not organized by willful control, but by a free and harmonious play of complementary forces, such as *yin and yang*, hot and cold, charge and discharge, flow and contraction, male and female, turmoil and stillness, chaos and order, and so on.

All those processes are self-executing, following an invisible program that is part of the unified field and highly complex. From the observation of these most basic functional mechanisms of nature, Reich derived healing methods for neuroses and sexual dysfunctions and new therapeutic approaches for schizophrenia and paranoia.

—Wilhelm Reich, The Schizophrenic Split (1945).

Later, Reich developed methods for healing major lifestyle diseases such as cancer, rheumatism, asthma, arthritis and leukemia.

—Wilhelm Reich, The Function of the Orgasm 2 (The Cancer Biopathy)(1948) and The Leukemia Problem (1951).

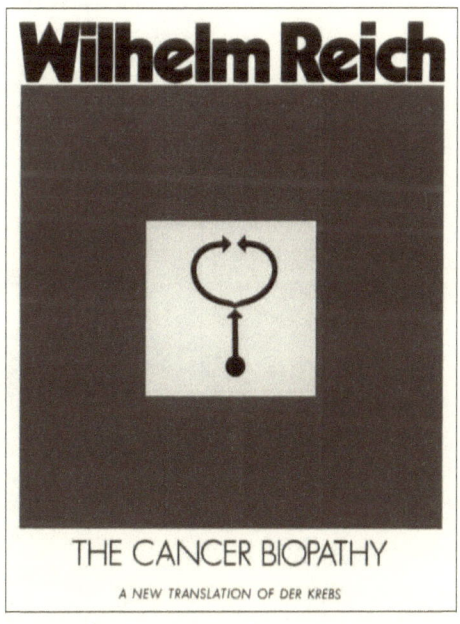

Reich used *self-regulation* to accelerate the pulsation of the bioplasma which, Reich found, was typically slowed down or even blocked with functional diseases. Through focusing on the *natural pulsation of the protoplasm during orgasm,* Reich came to the discovery of the bions and the orgone energy.

—What happens is that through the stimulation of the protoplasm which, during orgasm, gets for a short while into a kind of rhythmic pulsation, the plasma is charged with vital energy, see Wilhelm Reich, Function of the Orgasm (The Orgone Vol. 1)(1942).

THE LEUKEMIA PROBLEM:
APPROACH

WILHELM REICH

Orgone was a term Reich coined in order to denote the specific protoplasmic energy that he could see operating in the living, an observation that had started out with his *bion experiments* in which he had seen that orgone energy appears to be radiating as a blue phosphorescent light.

It is interesting to see how Reich and his assistants distilled bion-charged water. They merely would take sand from a beach, preferably sand that was exposed to the sunlight during a long time; then they would put this sand in a vacuum tube and burn it in a high-temperature oven; the ashes would then be mixed into distilled water.

Soon thereafter, the water would begin to radiate the bluish light which was visible when the laboratory was darkened.

Moreover, Reich found that when he remained an extended time in the room with the bion-charged water, his skin would slightly tan and he would feel high-spirited and light, as if he had been given an energy lift.

Soon Reich theorized that the energy he had just discovered probably was the *life force, ch'i* or *prana* that esoteric scriptures were vividly reporting and that was known to humanity since times immemorial.

Reich then concluded that he had found a biological confirmation of the psychoanalytic theory of neuroses. He was then able to conclude that an uninhibited and normal sexual function was the precondition for the orgonotic metabolism in the cell plasma and for the natural balance of the *ch'i* force or *élan vital.*

Reich had found empirical proof for the thesis that all so-called lifestyle diseases can be traced back to functional disturbances of the protoplasmic energy balance. This thesis, for traditional Chinese Medicine an old hat, was however revolutionary in a medical system that comes from vivisecting cadavers as its only way of understanding nature's functioning. The development of Reich's hypothesis until its verification in countless experiments and case reports makes the contents of Reich's most important book, his *Cancer Biopathy (1948)*.

DEFAMED YET CORROBORATED

However, academia not only ignored Reich's outstanding research, but slandered him, in much the same way as it did about a hundred years before him, with Franz Anton Mesmer. In fact, Mesmer came to similar results in his research on what he came to call *animal magnetism*.

—See Maria M. Tatar, Spellbound: Studies on Mesmerism and Literature (1978); Franklin Rausky, Mesmer ou la révolution thérapeutique (1977); Franz Anton Mesmer und die Geschichte des Mesmerismus (1985).

To make it worse, Reich was impersonated. He knew that a university colleague of his, Otto Fenichel, spread out the rumor Reich was paranoid. Although several reputed sources gave convincing testimony to the contrary, these rumors penetrated scientific circles on a worldwide scale and distorted public opinion to a point that the name Reich became anathema for every serious scientist.

Reich died in prison from a heart attack, in 1957! His books were publicly burned upon a court order. After his death, Reich's revolutionary findings were simply ignored by the majority of scientists!

His cancer biopathy was rediscovered only in the run of modern alternative cancer healing, after chemotherapy had effectively killed thousands of people so that medical science could uphold its claim that it can 'cure cancer.' The incredible cynicism of the modern cancer cure consists in the fact that as long as the patient died not of cancer but following a chemotherapy, the case was 'closed successfully.'

But only few of these alternative healers took a reference to Reich's pioneering work or simply plagiarized him, claiming the merits for their own assumed new therapies.

Only from about the 1970s Reich's research could gain recognition, in the trend of the general *liberalization of sexuality* and the public and scientific discussion of sexual matters. But until today, the number of people who really understand the totality of Reich's findings is infinitesimal. If we consider that, as early as in 1942, Reich has seen *ecological, sexual and political implications* of a complexity that we only get close to understand now, we can get a glimpse of his scientific genius. Where Freud only saw the symptoms, Reich found that the neurotic is generally incapable to surrender to the orgasmic convulsion and relaxation because of a muscular armor that, in turn, is but the somatization of a characterological armor.

Later research fully confirmed Reich's findings. Alexander Lowen, a New York based psychotherapist and early student of Reich equally found the same characterological patterns and chronic muscular spasms in sexually inhibited subjects, and developed Reich's bioenergetic approach further.

—See Alexander Lowen, Love and Orgasm (1965), Bioenergetics (1975), Pleasure (1970), Narcissism (1983), Fear of Life (2003).

The results of sexual dysfunctions are bioenergetic imbalances in a great number of people and, as a consequence, a collective worldview that is *deeply irrational.*

Based upon his insight in human character structure and the armoring mechanism, Reich took decisive conclusions as to the personality structure of the masses in industrial culture and found they suffer from a significant *lack of identity* which is compensated through the general infiltration of the mass media and material possessions.

Erich Fromm, although coming from a different angle, specialized on this part of the psychoanalytic research, and came to very similar conclusions.

—See, for example, Erich Fromm, The Anatomy of Human Destructiveness (1992), Escape from Freedom (1994), To Have or To Be (1996), The Art of Loving (2000).

A SCIENTIFIC GENIUS

Reich's merit consists in the discovery and formulation of something like a *total pathology of modern industrial culture* that is comprehensive also to lay people, while it is based on a bioenergetic, or, in his own terminology, *orgonotic* understanding of nature's complex interplay of opposing forces.

Reich concluded that there is a functional relationship between orgastic potency, personal independence, activity, creativity, political and religious tolerance, rationality, the recognition of women's and children's rights and democratic forms of government, on one hand, and orgasmic or sexual dysfunctions, fear of pleasure, authority craving, passivity and uncreative dullness, intolerance, fanatic irrationality and mysticism, the oppression of women and children and totalitarian forms of government, on the other. From the insights his sex research delivered, Reich lucidly explained the direct connection between psychological and political factors that are at the basis of the last five thousand years of human misery.

Only a few great contemporaries of Reich, such as J. Krishnamurti, explained the complex causes of the sickness of the human condition in a comparably holistic and comprehensive, however unscientific manner.

—See, for example, J. Krishnamurti, Freedom From The Known (1969), The First and Last Freedom (1975), Education and the Significance of Life (1978).

Sadly enough, it has to be seen that Krishnamurti, as so many great personalities from the so-called spiritual world in one or the other way tended to belittle the role of sexuality in human life and society.

—Krishnamurti went as far as declaring that he himself never had any sexual feelings. While he recognized the sexuality of the child and declared his educational approach to be non-judgmental as to children's emotional and sexual lives, de facto, as I know from meetings with several teachers from Krishnamurti Schools in England and India, this liberal approach is not practiced in Krishnamurti Schools for reasons of political correctness.

As early as in 1942, Reich wrote in *The Function of the Orgasm* that people who grow up impregnated with a generally negative attitude upon life and sexuality will develop a deeply rooted *fear of pleasure* that is characterologically anchored and somatized in form of a *corporal armor* that partly or totally suppresses their capacity to feel.

—This part of Reich's research and his insights about the collective fear of body pleasure in our culture has been fully corroborated, many years later, by Alexander Lowen, in his last book, Fear of Life (2003).

As a result, Reich found, these individuals will be easily affected and manipulated by life-denying philosophies and ideologies like fascism and tyrannical and totalitarian forms of government.

—Wilhelm Reich, Function of the Orgasm (1942), 7.

With regard to Freud's theory of a *death instinct*, Reich felt he had disproved its existence through clinical experiments. He wrote that he never encountered a will to die in any individual or patient. Psychic manifestations that could have indicated such a will or desire, had clearly been identified as *direct consequences* of sexual repression. (Id., 154-155)

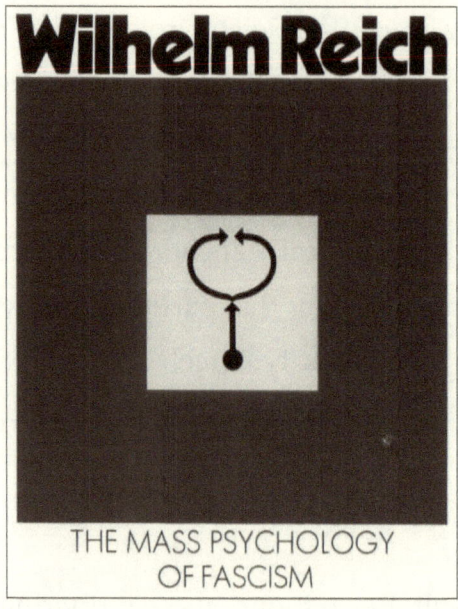

In further contradiction to Freud who erected the *preservation of culture* as the pillar of his psychoanalytical value system, Reich questioned the moralistic roof structure of modern culture and found it to be a life-denying system that distorts natural processes and thus perverts the human animal from early childhood.

Reich considered biogenic self-regulation as the only positive, healthy and evolutionary principle that a future society could and should be based upon. The principle of the natural regulation of the bioenergy, and the insight that sex-economy is a functional regulatory growth agent in all living are fundamental in Reich's research, and here he definitely is more rational-minded than Freud, and his research results markedly differ from Freud's cultural *moralism* in that they are scientifically repeatable and provable.

THE ROOT CAUSE OF VIOLENCE

Contrary to Freud's system, Reich's findings are based upon biological insights and not a merely mythical or conceptual rhetoric. As a result of his systemically sound research, Reich could find the real cause of antisocial acts; the etiology namely for those acts is nothing but *misdirected bioenergy* that flows out from a secondary drive structure; and by doing so he could largely disprove the older view that the human animal was violent, wrongly adjusted or perverted by nature. For Reich, human destructiveness is by no means inherent in human nature, as Freud and most religions assume, but a logical consequence of the *repression of natural life* and sexual functions in the moralistic social system.

> —Id., p. 7. Interestingly enough, the principle of self-regulation is equally the founding principle of the free market since this principle is valid not only biologically, but also in the social and commercial arenas. Furthermore, it can be said to be a character trait of every free and democratic human society.

These insights reflect the fact that Reich's entire research was much closer to the Eastern medical approach and to alternative natural healers such as Paracelsus who explain the functional logic of the organism in energetic terms and not in symptomatic categories.

This corroborates my view that Reich was the true founder of the *Aquarius Age*. Reich was the first medical doctor and bioenergy researcher to go beyond the inherent limitations of traditional medical science, and prepared the ground for the later integration of *acupuncture, intuitive diagnosis* and other *holistic and energy-based medical treatments* that fortunately are today part of the Western medical establishment.

> —See, for example, the contributions of Carolyn Myss and Barbara Ann Brennan in Russell DiCarlo, A New Worldview: Conversations at the Leading Edge (1996).

Reich attacked Freud's hypothesis that culture was the product of the *sublimation* of the instincts. Although Freud understood under sublimation not the repression but the integration of the instincts, Reich did not see an essential difference between sublimation and repression.

As later Masters & Johnson, Reich based his argument not upon mythological constructs, but upon clinical research. He found *sexual satisfaction* and not sexual 'sublimation' to be the source of all human creativeness, and also of all cultural achievements. Reich tried to prove that sexual repression has no biological basis but is a social and historical relict of civilization.

—Wilhelm Reich, The Function of the Orgasm (1942), 223.

Other of Freud's hypotheses were later disproved; for example, psychologists did not encounter signs of a sexual latency with freely raised children.

Similar observations were done by Alexander S. Neill in *Summerhill School* in England, and by two outstanding child sexuality researchers in the United States, Larry L. Constantine and Floyd M. Martinson.

—Alexander S. Neill, Summerhill (1960). See also Reich's Early Writings, Vol. 1 (1920-1925), Vol. 2 (1927), and Genitality in the Theory and Therapy of Neurosis (1980). Generally regarding the sexuality of children, see Larry L. Constantine & Floyd M. Martinson (Eds.), Children & Sex: New Findings, New Perspectives, Boston: Little, Brown & Company, 1981, Treasures of the Islands: Children in Alternative Lifestyles, Beverly Hills: Sage Publications, 1976, Floyd M. Martinson, Sexual Knowledge: Values and Behavior Patterns, St. Peter: Minn.: Gustavus Adolphus College, 1966, Infant and Child Sexuality, St. Peter: Minn.: Gustavus Adolphus College, 1973, The Quality of Adolescent Experiences, St. Peter: Minn.: Gustavus Adolphus College, 1974, The Sex Education of Young Children, in: Lorna

Brown (Ed.), Sex Education in the Eighties, New York, London: Plenum Press, 1981, pp. 51 ff., The Sexual Life of Children, New York: Bergin & Garvey, 1994, Children and Sex, Part II: Childhood Sexuality, in: Bullough & Bullough, Human Sexuality (1994), pp. 111-116.

For the future, Reich envisaged and claimed a fundamental change of societal attitudes in this respect.

There are sources of research corroborating Reich's thesis, among them Bronislaw Malinowski's field studies with the Trobriand natives in Melanesia. Observing the authoritarian patriarchal societal model and finding it characterized by either sadistic or masochistic tendencies in sexuality and social life, Reich concluded that once genital energies are frustrated, they become destructive.

—Wilhelm Reich, The Function of the Orgasm (1942), 159.

One of the most important aspects of Reich's research is his explanation of fascism.

—Wilhelm Reich, The Mass Psychology of Fascism (1933).

Reich put his research in a formula that says: sadistic brutality plus mysticism produces fascist mentality. He examined and quoted from defamatory pamphlets that Streicher, a member of the Hitler government, had published about Jews, in 1934, in

the *Stürmer*, the propaganda organ of the NSDAP.
This study served Reich to demonstrate a typical way
of how the Nazi regime attacked the Jews at the
beginning of the holocaust: they were publicly labeled
as *sex monsters*.

—Id., 245, with further references.

It seems that also today it is not a 'death instinct'
that lets the masses passively watch the preparation
of a global ecological and military catastrophe, but the
fact that the depersonalized mass man, as a
consequence of his *loss of intrinsic joy of life*, silently
postulates that life is suffering.

—See Jean Liedloff, The Continuum Concept (1977/1986).

It is for this reason that, as a matter of ignorance,
most people regard destructive collective
developments as fatally pre-programmed in human
destiny, with the result of course that, in fact, both
individual and collective responsibility for the
deterioration of human life and evolution are
persistently denied.

Advocacy for Child Sexual Rights

Reich was misunderstood, too, with respect to his
passionate advocacy for the *free sexuality of children*.

Churches and conservatives became his enemies for life; these institutions and groupings denied the existence of child sexuality while being obsessed with repressing it; they were thus utterly irrational about it. In fact, in the first decades of the 20th century, anti-masturbatory devices for small children were booming; physical violence against children, predominantly in religious institutions was rampant and for the most part unquestioned by psychiatry and police.

It was exactly this schizoid approach of the conservative strata in society that was for Reich the ultimate proof of the correctness of his characterological assessment of modern man.

While Reich, in his youth, actively worked for the liberalization of children's emotional life, he admitted later toward his close friend Alexander S. Neill, the founder of *Summerhill School,* that he was not sure if he could apply his orgasm theory to small children and babies.

—See Wilhelm Reich, Record of a Friendship (1981), 326-327.

However, Reich's doubt later became obsolete with Masters & Johnson's extensive sex research and the *Kinsey Report* corroborated Reich's hypothesis that healthy children are *fully orgasmic since birth*. In his last book, *Children of the Future (1950/1983)*, Reich traced the foundations of a new society that is based upon emotionally healthy child-rearing.

In this fragment, Reich lucidly discusses what later was confirmed by the research of scientists like James W. Prescott or Ashley Montagu, and specialists for alternative birth and integral health such as Frederick Leboyer and Michel Odent, that is, the re-discovery of the tactile needs of infants and their absolutely respectable desire for sensual pleasure.

—See Frederick Leboyer, Birth Without Violence (1975) and Loving Hands (1977) as well as Michel Odent, Birth Reborn (1986).

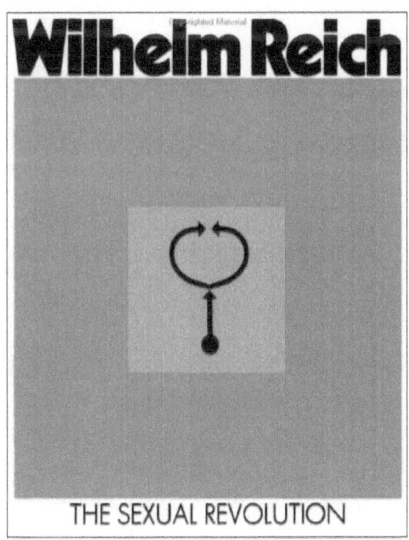

Implications

All of us, politicians, psychologists, lawyers, sociologists, therapists and educators are called upon to study and understand Reich's scientific heritage as there is nothing even remotely comparable to it. Reich's research is essential, if not a precondition for our present transformation of postmodern society and scientific culture, which is going to become more rational-minded, and eventually begins to acknowledge and integrate bioenergetic reality in the sociocultural and political realities of the human race, while formerly the life paradigm was based on fear, myth, custom, dogma, tradition, authority and irrationality.

While it is true that science still today does not recognize the *ether* and considers, for example, outer space as a vacuum, we cannot simplify matters to a point to say that the energy concept was alien to our culture. In fact, it was always present in both the Eastern and Western world, but it had to remain underground in the West because of the *denial of the tree of knowledge* as a result of the official dogma of the Christian Church that was enforced and upheld through the *Inquisition*. And yet, the alchemists and many branches of natural healing, especially the plant healers such as Paracelsus knew it all.

In all these different costumes, we see the same actor coming along: the *bioplasmatic cosmic life force* in its many masks and manifestations. We are dealing here with manifold ways and expressions for describing basically the same truth inherent in the function of living. While functional thinking about life and living was never distorted to that point in the East, in the West, through *moralism* and what Reich used to call the *emotional plague*, functional thinking and reasoning was relegated to an intellectual elite, while the masses still today are locked in a *hypertrophied intellectual perception of reality*; they are emotionally widely dysfunctional if not crippled through the still all-pervading taboo of natural sex for children and adolescents.

We cannot impudently act counter to the basic laws of the cosmos as we did during the past five thousand years of life-denying patriarchy, and the price we pay for this lack of respect and intelligence is high. We simply may perish as a race along the way!

The science of the bioenergy is also a new platform for *functional thinking* about life and society!

Wilhelm Reich was perhaps the first scientist in the West who was not only applying functional thinking in all his work, but who at the same time had the eminent pedagogical talent to explain to us the necessity to think functionally and not moralistically.

Reich reasoned that because *life* thinks functionally, we need to think in the same way, and not for any other reason. This simple answer leaves all religious and ideological fanatics in empty space— and that is where they belong, because they really do not have any ground under their feet, and their rants are simply irrelevant on the agenda of life.

We should begin to understand that the old controversy if creation was of a spiritual or material nature is a trap. This antinomy as part of civilization's thought structure is one of the *numerous artificial distinctions* that thought makes and that are not part of nature, as the intellectual mind is divisive while nature is *integrative*. Nature simply *is*. Creation *is*.

This *existential reality is energetic* and encompasses the whole landscape of life from the ethereal, highly fluctuant and all-pervasive that historically was called *ether* and now is called the *aura* or luminous body until dense and highly static matter like sand, stone or bones.

The notion of the ether that I have discussed earlier in this chapter is a quite catchy expression for something like an *energy and information field,* something that is not directly material like dense matter, but something that is ethereal. It is obvious that the adjective *ethereal,* as we use it for example in ethereal oil expresses something that lacks material substance and yet is full of substance.

And we could indeed explain the antinomy between spirit and matter as a mere function of the density of matter. As I showed above, Fritjof Capra remains vague on this point, while he correctly reflects and reports Reich's position, pointing out in *The Turning Point (1982/1987):*

> Reich saw this orgone research as some kind of primordial substance, present everywhere in the atmosphere and extending through all space, like the ether of the nineteenth-century physics. Inanimate as well as living matter, according to Reich, derives from *orgone energy through a complicated process of differentiation. (Id., 378)*

Interestingly enough, later in his book, when writing about the ancient Chinese concept of *ch'i,*

Capra also intelligently grasps the notion, but says the Western concept of ether could not adequately describe it:

> The concept of ch'i, which played an important role in almost every Chinese school of natural philosophy, implies a thoroughly dynamic conception of reality. The word literally means gas or ether and was used in ancient China to denote the vital breath or energy animating the cosmos. But neither of these Western terms describes the concept adequately. Ch'i is not a substance, nor does it have the purely quantitative meaning of our scientific concept of energy. It is used in Chinese medicine in a very subtle way to describe the various patterns of flow and fluctuation in the human organism, as well as the continual exchanges between organism and environment. (Id., 344)

The perhaps first researcher who understood that we are talking here about a *field* was Harold Saxton Burr. Still within the vocabulary of the old paradigm, but correctly observing the phenomenon, he called it an 'electrodynamic field,' and when these fields control living organisms, he called them *L-fields*. Georges Lakhovsky spoke of *resonance*; his insight in the resonant oscillations of cells, which is just another application and manifestation of the *L-field* enabled him to cure cancerous plants in various experiments.

Lynne McTaggart, in her thorough research on the matter published in her book *The Field (2002),* concluded that most science authors speak of the *zero-point field* when they denote the ether, or a mysterious invisible substance that already Capra recognized and intuited as not a substance in the strict sense, but something relating to *fields.*

There is no need to fight about words; all researchers coincide in the basic functionality of this substance that is actually no substance, but a *communication facilitator* in the universe. And the amazing thing about it is that this communication does not follow relativity theory as it's *instantaneous,* whatever the distance is between the two entities, particles, cells, molecules, plants, animals or humans that communicate with each other.

> —That is, by the way, how telepathy can be adequately explained today, and when the concept of the zero-point field is understood, it's implied that it would be sheer nonsense to speak in this and similar cases about speed, or communication 'surpassing the speed of the light.' There is no speed in telepathy. It's instantaneous. And the same is true, as Rupert Sheldrake points it out in his book A New Science of Life (2005), for morphic resonance, and it can be explained with basic principles of quantum mechanics.

The perhaps best researched and most lucid study written on the subject is Ervin Laszlo's book *Science and the Akashic Field (2004)*.

Laszlo presents the whole array of concepts and interpretations and tries to make out the break, the way a future science is going to apply and integrate these concepts in a *unified field theory* and an equally unified scientific vocabulary. And there is a high probability that Laszlo shows really the way we are going to go in the years to come.

Disappointing however is that his study mentions Wilhelm Reich with no word.

It is because of our separative mechanistic thinking over the past four hundred years of science that we have created problems in life that originally have no place in it and that the intuitively or emotionally intelligent thinker will not perceive as problems. An example for such an early holistic thinker is the German poet and scientist Johann Wolfgang von Goethe (1749-1832). Goethe's *pantheistic worldview* as well as his scientific discoveries such as his *color theory* that were rejected at his lifetime, would today be accepted in a science shattered and enriched by the endless paradoxes of quantum physics.

> —Johann Wolfgang von Goethe, The Theory of Colors (1810/1970) and Frederick Burwick, The Damnation of Newton: Goethe's Color Theory and Romantic Perception (1986).

Today, science is enriched with the essential insight that all matter, regardless or its density, is conscious; that is why the traditional scientific expression of 'inanimate nature' has become a misnomer. The universe is not empty as modern mainstream physics still assumes. It is filled, and totally filled, through and through, by the all-pervasive bioenergy that we may call as we wish, *orgone, prana, ch'i* or whatever, and that I call *e-force*. Ervin Laszlo speaks of a *plenum*, instead of a vacuum.

The next step ahead, without a doubt, will be the official recognition, scientific exploration and integration of the pattern-oriented science of the bioenergy, and the erudite study of its laws, that, as Reich has shown, are totally different from those that, for example, govern nuclear energy.

> —This hypothesis of Wilhelm Reich was eventually corroborated through a rather dangerous experiment in which Reich orgonotically charged Uranium. The experiment resulted in a catastrophe that led to the evacuation of Reich's orgone laboratory and private premises in Rangeley for several months. The incident is reported and discussed in two case reports by

Wilhelm Reich, The Oranur Experiment, First Report (1947-51), Orgone Institute Publications, 1951 and The Oranur Experiment, Second Report (1951-56), published in Contact With Space, New York: Pilot Press, 1957, to be ordered from the book store of the Wilhelm Reich Trust in Rangeley, Maine, USA.

Probably a new terminology will be created for this purpose that shall be different from the one used in esoteric literature since times immemorial, and probably also different from Reich's orgonomy research vocabulary.

As the trend is right now, there is a high probability that the universal bioplasmatic and cosmic energy will be described as a *field* that obeys to very specific laws, and therefore, quite intelligently, has been termed not energy, but *zero-point field*, *quantum vacuum, unified field* or *super-string field*, as the notion *energy* reminds kinetic energy and is as such really a misnomer.

One of the most important consequences of an official recognition of the bioenergy would be the levy of the ban over sexuality or certain forms of it that today are tabooed because society would have to recognize that sexuality in all its forms is *holy*, as it is itself the creator principle. This means that social paradigms would have to change, as well as criminal laws, and particularly the laws of consent, as I have shown in other publications.

And here we face perhaps the last and most persistent psychological blockage of perception that was the reason for Western science's persistent denial of the living energy within and without. Intuitively every natural scientist knows that all new discoveries in a so-called 'exact science' have an immediate impact on the moralistic roof structure of a given society's base paradigm of living.

To voice it clearly, an energy-conscious *functional science* will not uphold sex taboos; and such a science will inevitably impact on abolishing our ridiculous, outlandish and outright nonsensical sex laws. This is why until now a really functional and emotionally intelligent energy science has not yet been created; the reason simply is psychological and cultural resistance.

Orgonomy and Schizophrenia

It is of particular interest to have a closer look at schizophrenia, a look that disregards both the clichés of the past and those of our times. Science and medical science, as well as mental health care, are closely interrelated. It can be seen over the course of human scientific history that the paradigms that were considered as valid and relevant for science were equally applied for medical science and mental health care.

This close systemic connection between natural science and social sciences has been shown with exemplary clarity by Fritjof Capra in his book *The Turning Point (1982/1987)*.

In our postmodern culture, the transition from mechanistic to holistic science will have a sure impact upon social sciences in the sense that mechanistic approaches will be gradually replaced by mental health strategies that consider and integrate human values, and that will be effective on all levels, including the metarational, emotional and spiritual domains.

The remaining bastion, at the time of this writing, is *sexology*. Sexology is really the only science that so far has done no progress at all, that is still *completely mechanistic*.

Needless to add that this fact has devastating consequences, especially in *forensic psychiatry*, where the lack of professional insight in the connection between *emotions and organismic pleasure* led to the establishment of standard schemes that are used to inflict on so-called *sex offenders* draconian prison fines under the header of 'protecting the public of sexual assault.' The truth is that all violent sex is not the result of sexual attraction, but results from the very *repression* of that attraction.

Hence, a reform of sexology on the lines of the holistic science paradigm is badly needed, and even urgent. We cannot afford, as a society, to discard out larger and larger circles of the community simply because they haven't been able to handle their bioenergy at one or the other moment in their lives. For a change to happen here, we have to *reintegrate sexology into psychology and both into a real psychosomatic science* that encompasses both medical science and medical health practice.

While in the past, psychiatry was reductionist in recognizing only physiological reasons for mental disease, this has changed in the meantime—at least as far as the neuroses are concerned.

As early as in 1939, Carl Jung writes in his article *On the Psychogenesis of Schizophrenia (1993):*

There is little doubt nowadays about the
psychogenesis of hysteria and other neuroses,
although thirty years ago some brain enthusiasts still
cherished vague suspicions that at bottom 'there was
something organically wrong even with neuroses.'
But the consensus doctorum in their vast majority has
admitted the psychical causation of hysteria and
similar neuroses. (Id., 474-475)

While, for a large number of psychiatrists, this
view is still valid, Wilhelm Reich, as early as in 1945,
achieved complete healing of a schizophrenic patient
using orgonotic treatment.

Many a reader, and certainly mental health
professionals know about the ground-breaking work
of Ronald David Laing, Thomas Szasz and other
alternative psychiatrists for the treatment of *child
psychosis and schizophrenia.* However, small is the
number of individuals who have noticed that Reich's
research and mental health treatment approach by far
preceded those much more well-known and
acclaimed methods.

In fact, Reich achieved remarkable results with
simply liberating and integrating the patient's
internal bioenergy flow. Reich's schizophrenia
treatment seems revolutionary when we consider that

not long ago, Western psychiatry was barely anything more sophisticated than blunt torture.

For those who, like me, had a deeper look into alternative medicine, and the holistic energy principles of *Feng Shui*, Reich's holistic science approach and his cancer biopathy appear logical, systemically sound and effective. The truth about Reich is as easy and as difficult as the quest for truth about life itself. Most people in our culture are ignorant and have been held ignorant by first the ecclesiastical and today the economic power structures of a highly manipulatory society that regards the individual as a mere function-holder, not as a fully enlightened spiritual unit with full access to power, knowledge and wisdom.

The Energy Code

As long as we reduce living to a mere physiological or mechanical residue of survival functions, we cannot comprehend what is really going on in the human organism.

Chinese wisdom as an integral part of perennial science knows since more than five thousand years about the fundamental *energy code* of life. This knowledge was part of the great hermetic science that was shared in all ancient wisdom traditions. Reich rediscovered this truth for our modern times, using scientific tools and ways of analysis and observation, rather than philosophical reasoning. He built an enormous body of knowledge that today represents a bridge between the expanded holistic Eastern and our reductionist and fragmented science paradigms. While Carl Jung's psychogenesis of schizophrenia is mainly based upon Bleuler and the assumptions of Pierre Janet who sees the etiology of schizophrenia in a mere 'faiblesse de la volonté,' that is, a weakness of willpower resulting in a *reduction of mental abilities* or 'abaissement du niveau mental,' Reich really had tools at hand, and thereby created viable healing solutions because he penetrated through to the root cause of the disease.

Jung's article on schizophrenia, to be true, represents a literary and *somewhat philosophical* piece of writing without any practical or clinical corroboration. The sources Jung cites as a point of departure for his own approach appear unfit. In our times, Janet's view is absurd and it bears a strange taste of torture psychiatry.

During the old paradigm the 'madman' had to be considered as a lazy fool, an offender of society's normalcy standard, a human who got to be *not so human,* too weak to control himself and thus—following the Christian doctrine of the inherent immoral character of nature—a soul that regressed into indecent animal nature. *To be different from the norm was per se a crime.*

The *sex offender* or *perpetrator* is not considered as a human being and all human rights are denied to him as a result. From the literature, we know very well about the disastrous consequences of such thought-reforming outbursts of psychiatry that are now with the same cruelty applied to so-called *sex offenders*, and even *child sex offenders*, and we can only deplore that human intelligence is used in such diabolic and monstrous constructions when only the *Myth of Normalcy* is at stake.

Hitler Germany, Stalin's Soviet Union and Maoist China were perhaps extreme but in no way unique in their inhumanity towards people who bypass or defy the definitions of *normalcy*. Until today, in many countries, people who suffer from mental and emotional disturbances are beaten every day in mental health institutions.

Normalcy, as a concept and social standard, is the most dangerous idea humanity ever made up. It has been used to justify the worst of persecution, slander, intolerance, aggression and torture. And this went on to a point that even doctors, scientists who had acquired a high reputation for their work have been persecuted, slandered and, in Reich's case, even declared to be paranoid.

Today, we know and have the proof that these allegations against Mesmer and Reich were not true, but during their lifetime, it seems, most people succumbed to the peer pressure and violence of the ignorant majority.

The Schizophrenic Split

Before I read Jung's article on the psychogenesis of schizophrenia, I had studied Reich's case report of a successful yet difficult treatment of a schizophrenic patient. This report was not available in any bookstore and not even at Amazon's amazingly complete out-of-print collection. The only way to get it was to order a photocopy of the unpublished manuscript from the *Wilhelm Reich Trust* in Rangeley, Maine. As soon as I had read the first page, I was seized to a point that I could not stop reading.

While Jung's short article sets a milestone in giving sound reasons to discard the physiological etiology and adopt the psychic etiology of schizophrenia, Reich's contribution takes a perspective not comparable to anything that has been written or practiced on schizophrenia ever before in the West.

Reich's approach to schizophrenia can only be fully understood if one is familiar with Reich's revolutionary treatment of neuroses and his discovery of the orgone and, as a consequence, the insight into the characterological and muscular armoring that takes place in neuroses and, even more so, in psychoses.

To summarize Reich's discoveries and revolutionary treatment approach very shortly, let me just list the main features of his approach to holistic healing and then explain them briefly—

—Mental illness is a *distortion of perception* resulting from a blockage of the emotional flow;

—Neuroses and psychoses are the result not of mental or intellectual but of *emotional and psychosexual disturbances* suffered early in life; more precisely, they are the results of early infringement in the natural emotional flow caused by moralistic education; this infringement consists in the social or cultural impeachment of discharging the emotional and sexual energies through orgasm;

—Treating neuroses and psychoses is difficult because what needs to be done is to alter the polarity of accumulated negative energy, or DOR, in Reichian terms; more precisely, DOR or 'deadly orgone' accumulates in the plasma creating a characterological and muscular armoring that transforms the afflicted into negative, life-denying, mystic and irrational people. Reich called this process the *emotional plague;*

—Reich's healing approach does not use traditional psychoanalysis because of its body-touch taboo, while Reich saw the body as the entry point to the healing of the psychic affliction; healing is effected by dissolving the muscular armor bit by bit through the Reichian deep tissue massage;

—Reich construed the *Orgone Energy Accumulator,* a device made from several layers of wood, isolator material and copper plates that serves to accumulate the natural atmospheric orgone in order to help the patient absorb cosmic energy into their bioplasmatic system by sitting one or two hours daily in the box;

—Reich also developed special shooters that work similarly and can be used ideally while sitting in the accumulator, pointing the shooter to the neuralgic point in the body for immediate relief of pain and healing;

—From his body work, Reich came to observe the flow of the *atmospheric orgone,* just as the old sages did thousands of years ago, and could explain phenomena hitherto unknown such as *aurora borealis* or desertification;

—Reich developed a special *cloud buster,* a mechanical device consisting of metal tubes erected toward the sky that are connected via thick copper cables into ground water; with this device Reich achieved bringing about rain or stopping rain at will; again, this almost miraculous impact on the atmospheric orgone was in accordance with what already the sages of old, and Tibetan lamas, knew and practiced, only with the difference that they could bring about the weather-altering effects *telepathically* and through prayer, while Reich needed a mechanical device;

—Reich described in a voluminous dossier the existence of UFOs and CORE men (extraterrestrials) and delivered abundant proof of his observations in various lengthy reports part of which he submitted to the US Air Force for investigation and corroboration.

Wilhelm Reich's research has broken ground for present researchers to understand that the core life function is primarily an *energy field function* and not a question of manipulating matter—as it was seen under the old Newtonian science paradigm. It is therefore of particular importance how Reich treated successfully an affliction as devastating and as difficult to heal as schizophrenia.

It appears that this success was due not only to Reich's lucidity as a therapist, but also to his understanding and compassion for the patient. Reich's attitude is markedly different from the somewhat distant and slightly cynical observations of Carl Jung on the subject of schizophrenia. Reich's short introduction in the case study shows empathy and understanding of the situation of the patient that are really unparalleled in psychiatric literature:

> The idea of the devil is a true expression of the distortion of nature in man. No other human experience lends itself as well as the schizophrenic

experience to the study of the devil. The schizophrenic world in its purest form is a mixture of mysticism and emotional inferno, of penetrating though distorted vision, of God and devil, of perverse sex and murderous morals, of sanity to the highest degree of genius and insanity to its deepest depth, welded into a single horrible experience.

—Wilhelm Reich, The Schizophrenic Split (1945), 1.

I do not know a single therapist who penetrated with equal lucidity the deeply mystic experience of mental illness; from what Reich writes, we can understand that the irrational denial of understanding schizophrenia is a sort of professional handicap in psychiatry.

Another topic often discussed within the antipsychiatry movement and similar forums are the obvious parallels between *madness and genius,* a phenomenon that is often bluntly misunderstood, but which is a confusing element especially in schizophrenia.

Salvador Dali is known to have said that the only difference between Dali and a madman is that 'Dali is not a madman.' Apparently, many elements in Dali's art, and in surrealism in general connote mental disturbance, but only if one sees it that way.

One could see it as a way of *perceiving reality differently*, or as the attempt to penetrate into parallel realities; or one could question the very concept of an objective reality and conclude as to the existence of *subjective reality*, and individual creation of reality. Reich points out the difference between a schizophrenic and the exceptionally gifted, and he is very outspoken about the signs of mental distortion:

> The schizophrenic world mingles in one experience what is kept painstakingly separate in homo normalis. The well-adjusted homo normalis is composed of exactly the same type of experiences as the schizophrenic. Depth psychiatry leaves no doubt about this. Homo normalis differs from the schizophrenic only in that these functions are differently arranged. (Id., 2)

In my work with *voice dialogue* I came to exactly the same conclusion.

—See Peter Fritz Walter, Walter's Inner Child Coaching: A Guide for Your Inner Journey (2015/2017).

Actually, during that time and within that self-therapy I was prone to high anxiety and some form of regression and resulting ego dissolution through various practices of meditation, fasting and other techniques conducive to self-transformation. We can in fact pass healthily through various phases of mental disturbance if only—and this is the decisive point—we maintain a *residue amount of mental and emotional balance* that enables us to remain the observer of what is going on.

Once this observer which is part of the ego or identity, is dissolved, alien forces, spirits or whatever can penetrate in our psychic landscape, and the result then is most likely some form of psychosis or personality split.

The good thing to have passed through all that healthily and recovering from the anxiety has given me the privilege to *understand what a psychotic or schizophrenic mind is going through* and to what extent such a person is tortured.

In ancient times, these extreme forms of mental disturbance were considered as punishments by the Gods, and this view still prevails in earth-bound cultures. And there may be some truth in it. The I Ching points this out in the 21st hexagram, and the Tarot de Marseille in the 16th Arcane, and if we take an analogy to Greek mythology, we discover that the legend of King Minos of Crete expresses it in still another form. And then we've got Hamlet ...

Since childhood I knew that poets are closer to truth than other humans and certainly closer than most so-called mental health professionals. Most professionals today live in mental prisons, and they exclude more knowledge than they can assimilate, and thus keep their world hermetically closed by means of their professional associations, brotherhoods, circle of friends, social environment, and so on.

I have broken free from all of these prisons; they were but temporary lodgings for me. Today I do not belong to any professional circle and feel I can see the truth in myself and others more clearly while still doing those activities and being this or that for those who think one had *to be and to become* in order to 'represent something' in the world.

While my interest in Reich's research dates back to my early times at law school when I began devouring his books, it was only many years later that I realized how *systemically sound* this exceptional queer doctor was, and how many of his revolutionary discoveries have formed part of perennial wisdom. At a time when quantum physics was not yet popular, Reich was one of the few scientists who acknowledged that there is nothing observed without the observer being involved in some or the other way.

Throughout human history, we can observe that those who were rejected as *offenders* most of the time did not offend anybody. Their tragedy was that they did not fit into the behavior codex and thus defied the custom settings of their culture's root program. The truth is that these people are the scapegoats of the masses because they stand for a higher vintage of truth, being simply themselves truthful, without playing the 'me too' game.

Psychologically, the process is easy to understand once we grasp the concept of *projection*. Projection occurs when we deny parts of ourselves that we do not accept or that we are afraid of; what then happens is that those blind spots in us disappear from our wake consciousness, to get repressed into our subconscious mind. As a result, we project those characteristics, desires, traits or behavior patterns onto others and construe a belief system that secures us from re-discovering the truth that we have decided to hide from ourselves.

When this happens on a larger scale, social tolerance gets lost in the process and more and more scapegoats have to be slaughtered for society to maintain their shallow and life-denying setup. All this, we know it, but few of us really act upon this truth! Among those who do are the so-called schizophrenics.

Reich remarks several times in his study that typically schizophrenics are hated for their outspokenness, their lack of tact, their bluntness in saying ugly things that we all try to hide from the surface of our daily routines, but that we know are true. Thus they trigger the projection process in the majority in that they often point the finger on the wound, telling people their most carefully hidden thoughts, because they perceive other people's thoughts intuitively. And this behavior is then interpreted as 'aggressiveness' rather than as what it truly is: an attempt to opening up a deeper form of exchange, a more truthful and rewarding one than what is the usual hypocrite way of dealing with each other in 'civilized' society. Of course, their disturbance makes it often impossible for them to be listened to without apprehension, without suspicion or estrangement—and that is their very tragedy. But in trying to understand them, we are down the road going to better understand ourselves and the world as it is, and we can question so many of our false friends, inside and outside. Reich lucidly comments:

> The fact is that the schizophrenic is, on the average, much more honest than homo normalis, if one accepts directness of expression as an indication of honesty. Every good psychiatrist knows that the schizophrenic is embarrassingly honest. He is also what is commonly called deep, i.e., in contact with happenings. The schizoid person sees through hypocrisy and does not hide the fact. He has an excellent grasp of emotional realities, in sharp contradistinction to homo normalis. I am stressing these schizophrenic characteristics in order to make comprehensible why homo normalis hates the schizoid mind so much. (Id., 3)

Before I am going to discuss the case report in detail, I shall provide some further explanation on the subject of the Reichian *bioenergetic healing technique.* This is so much the more indicated as Reich's approach to psychic health is fundamentally different from psychoanalysis. Reich himself points this out at the beginning of his case study:

> The psychoanalytic arrangement of mental functions according to the three great realms of the ego, the superego, and the id has to be sharply distinguished from the biophysical arrangement of the functions of

the total organism according to the functional realms of bioenergetic core (plasma system), periphery (skin surface), and orgone energy field beyond the body surface. These two theoretical structures describe different realms of nature in a different manner. Neither is applicable to the other realm of organismic functioning. There is only one meeting point of the two theoretical schemata, i.e., the id of psychoanalytic theory, where the realm of psychology ends and that of biophysics beyond psychology begins. (Id., 5)

Those who are trained in Freudian psychoanalysis often misunderstand or belittle the Reichian healing method, or it is argued that it was immoral or against the rules of the art to touch the patient's body. In fact, to take a critical perspective, it appears that Freudian psychoanalysis more or less denies the existence of the patient's body and therefore takes a much longer way to access the core problem.

The way a Freudian analyst works is deprived of emotions. Symptomatically, it is considered inappropriate to show emotion from the side of the analyst. The Freudian therapist suggests to the patient's subconscious that he better not shows emotions, thus being 'rational all the time.'

What happens is that the whole therapy passes more or less through the left brain and becomes a kind of intellectual exercise or mind game; the interaction between analyst and patient is primarily linguistic and does not directly imply emotions, let alone tactile cognition.

This is one of the reasons why the Freudian psychoanalytic approach is rather time-consuming until any betterment is achieved—let alone complete healing, which is more often than not reported to be the exception rather than the rule.

To repeat it, the break between Reich and Freud occurred when Reich started sex research. Freud did not welcome *The Function of the Orgasm* and uttered that Reich's work offended the culture.

Today, if we ask which approach to healing emotional or mental disease is effective, the answer is without a doubt that it's the Reichian method. Reich rightly attacked Freud's assumptions, pointing out that a merely linguistic therapy can never effectively deal with the emotional and somatic core problem that is at the root of the neurotic symptoms.

In Freudian therapy, the emotional scars that cause the disturbance are circumvented and appear through associations and dreams. The picture may be clear for the analyst but it may remain strangely hidden to the patient himself or herself. This is totally different in the Reichian way of healing emotional diseases. Reich early recognized that since the core problem is always related to emotions and emotional energy, the healing can only occur through accessing and redirecting the emotional flow. It is this energy that feeds the symptoms. Reich put it that way:

> The most effective therapeutic approach to any emotional (biophysical) disease is, if at all possible or indicated, the withdrawal of bioenergy from the biopathic symptoms. In order to destroy psychoneurotic or psychotic symptoms it is unnecessary and even harmful to delve into all details of the countless pathological ramifications; instead, opening up the core of the biosystem and establishing *a balanced energy economy will automatically make the symptoms disappear,* since, seen energetically, they are results of a disorderly energy metabolism in the biosystem. (Id.)

It is difficult for most of our health professionals to think in terms of *subtle energy* and to acknowledge the streaming of the bioenergetic flow in all living, be it in our bioplasma or the atmosphere. This is in part due to our Judeo-Christian heritage which early denied the existence of subtle energies; nature and natural functions were considered a threat to the life-denying doctrine of monotheism with all its clear-cut nonsense about life.

The sages of old and Taoism acknowledged what today we call bioenergy and the existence of a *subtle* or hidden truth that cannot be grasped through a personified or materialized form named 'God' or otherwise. Consequently, those sages were really perfect healers because they knew how to realign the bioplasmatic charge and the balance of *yin and yang* according to the original setup that nature has coded into life. They could heal with simply laying on hands or they used plants or massage techniques for healing. Taoism forbade to open the body, so operations were not carried out.

We know from various sources that in ancient China cancer was healed solely by means of a *deep tissue massage technique* very similar to the one Wilhelm Reich rediscovered for our times.

What this massage does is to gradually dissolve the muscular armor of the patient so that the energy clusters that are frozen in the armor can be stimulated and opened so that the energy is fed into the emotional flow; the ancient sages would say that the *ch'i* is renewed.

This technique is difficult to learn, and it requires full emotional maturity on the side of the therapist. It is not without danger. Reich warns:

> Great danger arises in neurotics as well as in psychotics when the armor begins to dissolve. Utmost caution and medical skill are required to guide this process. The practice of medical orgone therapy is therefore restricted to well-trained physicians. We know our responsibilities better than anyone else and we do not have to be reminded of them by people who know little about orgonomy. (Id., 5)

After these preliminary notes, I would like to begin discussing the case study and my attention shall be focused on the question how Reich was able—to use his own words—to 'remove the psychic energy from the symptoms' that are specific disturbances in schizophrenia and to redirect this energy into the natural orgonotic energy flow of the patient's organism. To repeat, the point of departure in Reich's healing approach is bioenergetic, not psychoanalytic. Reich states:

> Our approach to schizophrenia is a biophysical, and not a psychological one. We try to comprehend the psychological disturbances on the basis of the plasmatic dysfunctions; and we try to understand the

cosmic fantasies of the schizophrenic in terms of the functions of a cosmic orgone energy which governs his organism, although he perceives his body energy in a psychotically distorted manner. (Id., 35)

This is very important to stress in order to avoid misunderstandings. It would be highly misleading to say that Reich treated schizophrenia psychoanalytically. I am convinced, not only because of the scarce contribution of Carl Jung cited above that *psychoanalysis cannot successfully cure schizophrenia.*

Without understanding the bioenergetic streaming in the human organism, Reich would not have been able to heal schizophrenia. It was his breaking away from psychoanalysis and his discovery of the muscular and characterological armors that enabled Reich to look at mental illness in a new and revolutionary way; it was his experience as a physician much more than his knowledge about psychology.

Doing this, Reich situated his healing approach on an equal level with the old Chinese healers who directly manipulated the subtle energies, and he successfully put a distance between his healing approach and the ridiculously limited efforts of modern medicine. That is, in my view, the main reason that his contemporaries, and especially his medical colleagues viciously attacked him!

I am quite sure that artists and people who know intuitively about the subtle truth of the bioenergy, such as spiritual healers, understood him much better.

When a Chinese doctor or a Tibetan healer approach a sick person, the first two things they check are the pulse and the breath. A well-trained Tibetan doctor can diagnose a disease years in advance simply by listening attentively to the pulse and, putting his ear and hands on the chest of the patient, listening and feeling if the breath is shallow or deep and diaphragmatic.

Here is what Reich stated when, during the first session of the treatment, he diagnosed the patient's physical condition:

> She seemed not to breathe at all. On physical examination her chest appeared soft, not rigid as in cases of compulsion neurosis. This softness and mobility of the chest were later found in other initial schizophrenics. It should be further investigated whether and to what extent the lack of armoring in the chest is or is not a characteristic of the schizophrenic biopathy. (Id., 8)

It appears that Reich, while not being sure about all the details, was really putting the finger on the wound. There was a paradox. The chest was not armored yet the patient did not breathe deeply. That did not seem to make sense. And it was later this paradox, as it is so often in science, that led Reich to the solution of the riddle.

The interesting thing is that this case was Reich's first attempt to heal schizophrenia, and he was well aware of the challenge. Reich pursues:

> When I asked the patient to inhale and exhale audibly, she refused; it was later shown that she was unable to do it. She seemed to stop the respiration somewhere in the cervical segments. (Id., 9)

This first observation at the beginning of the treatment was very important. Yet it seemed somewhat insignificant or would have seemed so to any other physician but Reich. Indeed, even the layman reader may reflect a moment on this somewhat strange behavior. Why should a person be unable to breathe deeply if it was not a muscular problem, a stiffness in the body? If the body is supple and flexible, why should the person not move the diaphragm to inhale and exhale? Could there be anything on a psychic or involuntary level that would hold a person from breathing rightly and deeply?

This first question was exactly the question a Chinese or Tibetan or any natural healer would have asked, and not only in cases of mental illness, but in every case of illness.

Western medicine, on the other hand, used to violate the patient rather than helping them to collaborate in the healing, ignorant of the true roots of life and consequently of the effective possibilities to bring about healing.

Our medical tradition, especially since Louis Pasteur, was obsessed with microbes, malefic bacteria, fixated upon the rotten, the dead, the pestilent, rather than upon the healthy and natural, the stamina of life.

Reich, by contrast, took a *pro-life approach*; he was optimistic that he could heal the patient, but he was careful. He knew if he'd go too fast, he would not only miss the chance of a true healing, but even endanger the patient. To counter this danger, Reich used a therapeutic technique that intelligently and flexibly combined somatic and intellectual interaction, resulting in both body and mind being involved in the healing.

Until the sixth session, Reich had to acknowledge
that he was still right at the beginning of the
treatment. It was then, and only then, possible to
penetrate to a deeper level of the patient's personal
history and to get her to remember events during
puberty. He writes:

> She realized that she held on to reality only with
> great effort; she had felt as though she were hanging
> over an abyss most of the time, especially during
> puberty. (Id., 12)

I know from my own experience with
psychotherapy that the care every good therapist
takes at the onset of the therapy is the condition for
the later success of the treatment. Reich stresses this
point in his report of the eighth session with the
patient:

> It is an important rule in disarmoring people to
> proceed slowly, step by step, and not to advance
> further into the biophysical depth unless one knows
> exactly what is going on and unless the patient has
> become accustomed to the situation which has
> already been reached. This is valid for all types of
> medical orgone therapy; it is especially necessary in
> the treatment of schizoid characters. (Id., 14)

No wonder why there is so little success in healing mental illness if we consider the *aggressiveness and brutality that surrounds mental institutions* and that is since centuries in our culture the standard in treating mental illness. Reich revolutionized this whole system and his writings unveil how exceptional such a new approach would be in the still highly violent environment of mental health care today.

But perhaps the most important is the role that *respect* plays in the whole of the interaction between the psychiatrist and his patient.

Informed professionals, if they care at all, may know the great work of alternative psychiatrists such as Ronald David Laing, co-founder of the antipsychiatry movement.

But Reich long preceded that event and practiced it patiently and despite all the hatred he had to sack in for being too different, too daring and, yes, too lucid—and this very lucidity was held against him as a sign of his own presumed mental illness.

Reich understood the schizoid character not because he himself was schizoid but because he was naturally compassionate and intelligent enough to be able to penetrate into the situation of another and to perceive the tragedy of another's life. Reich stated in the eighth session:

> Schizophrenics are able in their lucid periods to see through individual and social matters intelligently, as no other character type can. Later we shall see that this lucidity of intelligence in the schizophrenic is one of the major dangers which threaten his existence in present-day society. (Id., 15)

Respect, care and understanding are the foundation that the schizoid patient needs for building trust with the healer. Without trust, the chance of healing is *minimized to zero* from the very start of the therapy. The lack of trust between patient and psychiatrist is probably the main reason for the misery in most of our mental institutions, and not lacking knowledge, not a lacking number of staff and all the rest of pretexts that are commonly forwarded by professionals to cover up the truth about mental illness in our society. The lack of effectiveness in mental health care is primarily due to the lack of respect, the violence and brutality that this society inflicts upon those who are different from its rosy foam of *normalcy*. In addition, the presumed clear-cut distinction between mental health and mental disease does not exist. The borderline is a grey area that is defined differently by mental health professionals, mental health schools or methods or social environments, or cultures.

Reich, commenting on what his female patient called *The Forces,* that is, the voices she more or less unwillingly followed, comments:

> In contradistinction to the schizophrenic structure, the structure of homo normalis keeps one or the other of the contradictory structures continually in a state of repression. Thus, in homo normalis, the split of the personality is hidden. (Id., 17)

If we take Reich's social diagnosis serious, we come to realize that schizophrenia is *not a mental disease,* but a cultural pathology. If we are all schizoid because of the denial of our true nature in an upside-down society, we indeed only differ from the schizophrenic in that we hide this inner split, this dualism, this deep fragmentation, whereas the schizophrenic, essentially more daring, more honest and perhaps more intelligent than we are, openly unveils and expresses it. Of course, there were and are psychiatrists who have respect of the schizophrenic; some of these doctors said that every madman is a saint. Reich states:

Therefore, let us be reasonable; let us abandon our false righteousness. There must be a potent reason why the schizophrenic is treated so cruelly and the cruel homo normalis is honored so crazily all over the planet. (Id., 19)

Reich was perhaps the only scientist and medical doctor who, in our culture, has shown and openly expressed his wound, his shame and his indignation about the suffering of the human nature in our society. If we did not know who he was, we may take him as a peace apostle—and I mean this absolutely in the positive and innocent sense of the word. After all, he has written a book entitled *The Murder of Christ,* while he was not a pastor or theologian; he was agnostic but practiced the only right and natural form of religion which is *compassion with suffering*. He wrote:

> We must try instead to understand it when the schizophrenic expresses rational functions in a distorted manner. Therefore, it is necessary to judge him from beyond this orderly world of ours; we must judge him from his own standpoint. This is not easy. But if one penetrates the distortions, a wide vista opens up on a vast realm of human experience, rich in truth and beauty. It is the realm from which all the great deeds of genius emerge. (Id., 21)

Accompanying the patient during her regression into childhood, Reich found the repression of early childhood sexuality to be the *primary reason* for the characterological armor; he thus saw his theory confirmed that child sexuality is a necessity for psychic health. He comments:

> Such armoring usually results from cruel punishment for quite innocent behavior in childhood. (Id., 20)

But it was not before the 11th session that Reich really understood what was going on in his patient. Again and again, his conclusions were overthrown by the patient, again and again what seemed to have been achieved in trying to understand her, seemed to melt away like a foolish error or a frantic idealistic idea that had no true reality. The results that Reich could book positively seemed minimal compared to the constant drawbacks that occurred during this treatment that went over about two years. One or two of those drawbacks could have been fatal for the outcome of the therapy and the danger of suicide of the patient was imminent during the whole of the treatment.

The red thread that led Reich and his patient through the process, the only thing they could count upon was what happened on a feeling level with the patient; insofar there was a slow, very slow progress. What happened was that the patient had come in touch with her feelings, and this contact turned out to be the golden key for the later healing.

However, Reich knew this only intuitively at the start and he was not sure that this was really the most important part of the treatment. It was only after the eleventh session that his intuition had reached a kind of condensation and confirmation so that he could summarize the results in the following three points:

> During this session, the prospects of her therapy had become clear: The more and better contact she made with her plasmatic, bioenergetic streaming sensations, the less the fear of the forces would be. This would also prove my contention that the forces in schizophrenia are distorted perceptions of the basic orgonotic organ sensations. / This contact with her body sensations would help to establish some degree of orgastic satisfaction, and this in turn would eliminate the energy stasis which operated at the core of her delusions. (...) The undistorted experiencing of her body sensations would enable her to identify the true nature of the forces and would thus slowly destroy the delusion. (Id., 24-25)

However, the goal was not yet reached. Actually only the first step was made. Point two and three were only expectations, logical perhaps, but nonetheless unreal at the present state of the treatment. Reich had no illusions as to the further steps to be taken and as to the drawbacks that might occur along the way:

> Before this could be accomplished, the patient would have to pass through a series of dangerous situations. Delusions and catatonic reactions were to be expected with each breakthrough of strong orgonotic streamings in her body. She would perceive these sensations with terror; she would block them off by bodily rigidity, and the blocked off plasmatic currents would be transformed into destructive impulses. Therefore, the secondary impulses, which derive from the blocking of the original, basic emotions, would have to be handled carefully and would have to be let out slowly, step by step. This danger would become especially great when the first spontaneous orgastic contractions of her organism began to occur. (Id.)

With this turn, the therapy entered an abyss and the story, as most of Reich's treatment stories, became more of a frantic thriller than a case report. The patient had committed a suicide attempt shortly after the session, yet was saved in the very last moment. She had hurt herself badly with a razor, but quickly recovered. The more Reich opened her bioenergetic channels, the more deadly orgone (DOR) was set free in her organism and the usual love-hate confusion and accompanying aggressiveness against her therapist began to develop in the patient. Reich knew about this complex and somewhat dangerous process from the start, and he naturally focused upon its positive part, that is, the liberation of the patient's natural orgonotic streaming. Yet he was aware that the life-denying education and all the self-hate of the patient would make this process a difficult one with many drawbacks. He comments:

> We have seen how the sweet, melting organ sensations, the most longed for experience in the organism, are dreaded and fought off as brutal flesh in the sense of homo normalis and as evil forces or the devil in the psychosis. (Id., 27)

I think Reich was only logical to have drawn conclusions from the observations of the individual suffering that pertain to a more collective level, or to humanity as a whole. He writes:

I would like to stress this structural function of the armored human animal most empathetically. To the biopsychiatrist with long experience in orgone therapy, this dichotomy and ambivalence toward one's own organism appears as the crux of the misery of the human animal. It is the core of all human functions which are deviations from the natural law of living matter. It is the core of criminal behavior, psychotic processes, neurotic dreadness, irrational thinking, of the general basic split into the world of God and the world of the devil in human intellectual existence. What is called God turns into the devil by exactly / these distortions of living functions, i.e., by the denial of God. In the schizophrenic, these natural functions as well as their distortions appear in quite an undisguised manner. One has only to learn to read the schizophrenic language. (Id., 27-28)

If we read the schizophrenic language of many a journalist, we may realize how deeply the schizoid mindset is part of our culture, part of our so-called civilization that is haunted by obsessions, fears and collective hysteria.

Reich was aware of the social and political implications of his research and he had to face persecution, first, since he was of Jewish origin, from the Nazis in Germany who forced him to flee to Denmark, Norway, and finally America; but he was even more dangerously attacked from the side of fascist circles within American culture. With his usual lucidity he comments:

> Since nobody but the human animal himself has created his philosophies of life and his religions, it must be true that whatever dichotomies appear in ideologies and thinking stem from this structural split with its insoluble contradictions. (Id., 28)

A doctor who draws *political conclusions from his clinical observations* is necessarily a disturbing force in a society that invests tremendous energy in hiding its wound and its shame. However, Reich's side remarks did not prevent him from focusing on the therapy and they represent add-ons to his strictly medical observations and conclusions. Back on commenting on the therapy, he writes:

> It occurs regularly that the patient despises the therapist when the orgonotic streamings break through; this happens in all cases, including neurotics; it is a quite typical reaction. It corresponds to the hate and disdain shown by impotent, armored individuals toward healthy people and genital sexuality; usually, anti-Semitic ideas / occur at this point, in the Jew as well as in the non-Jew. The disdain usually centers around the idea that the

therapist, who deals with natural genitality, must be a sexual swine. (Id., 31-32)

Taking account of these shortcomings in orgone therapy, it becomes easier to understand why Reich's remarks so often reach a *cultural, social* or *political* level. In fact, individual and collective aspects of schizophrenia must be seen together, for nothing happens in a sociopolitical vacuum and things are connected as microcosm and macrocosm are essentially two realms of one single reality. A society of humans that have a schizoid predisposition because of life-alienating structures in child-rearing and the brutal or subtle *repression of the child's natural sexual emotions* cannot be expected to be other than schizoid. Such a society, at least when controversial matters are at stake, will react in a schizoid manner. Reich writes:

> Homo normalis does not understand this remoteness and is apt to call it crazy. He calls psychotic what is foreign to him, what threatens his mediocrity. (Id., 32)

Reich clearly observed with schizophrenics that their intelligence is above average and that they are unusually honest, bold and queer. He concluded that they have in common to refuse accepting the general hypocrisy of human civilization that the adapted citizen doesn't question and that, contrary to the neurotic or sadistic character, the schizophrenic is in touch with natural energies, albeit in a distorted manner. Reich writes:

> But the expression of the eyes is deep in both cases, and not flat, empty, sadistic or dull as in neurotic characters who have no contact with their bioenergy at all. (Id., 32)

Hence, the schizophrenic is a *borderline character* between the neurotic/sadistic and the healthy genital character.

Reading Reich, I gain the impression that the schizophrenic is closer to the genital character than the neurotic or the sadist are.

> Thus, a schizophrenic will fall into a state of disorientation when his self perception is overwhelmed by strong sensations or orgonotic plasma streamings; the healthy genital character will feel well, happy, and highly coordinated under the impact of orgonotic streaming. (Id., 35)

Orgonotic streaming is locked in the neurotic and even more in the sadistic character because of the strong muscular armor that inhibits the body of these individuals from yielding to the natural streaming of their hot melting sensations during the three phases of sexual excitation, before, during and shortly after orgasm.

Neurotics and sadists are emotionally cold and they tend to repress and deny the *whole of their feeling level;* they experience orgasm as a power thrust, a way to dominate others, a satisfaction derived from the pleasure to subdue, to control and to overpower another.

Unfortunately Reich was facing aggressive silence and unwilling resistance from the part of his colleagues since he seemed to consider the schizophrenic 'more normal' than the neurotic. Of course, to boil things down in such a simplistic way only leads to superficial conclusions. Reich did actually not make a judgment about this matter, and he was unjustly confronted with an attack from the side of traditional psychiatry. Yet he never belittled schizophrenia and was many times facing criminal behavior from the side of patients, and sometimes he even risked his life. But he had a sound explanation for *dementia,* and we have seen earlier on that, for example, Jung, had none. Reich stated:

The general deterioration of the organism in later phases of the process is due to chronic shrinking of the vital apparatus, as in the cancer biopathy, though different in origin and function. The shrinking carcinomatous organism is not in conflict with social institutions, *due to its resignation.* The shrinking schizophrenic organism is full of conflicts with the social pattern to which it reacts with a specific split. (Id., 36)

Nobody but Reich saw the similarity between cancer and schizophrenia in that they both are *hidden forms of slow suicide* that is preceded by giving-up fighting (cancer) or by too much fighting (schizophrenia) against the life-denying system that represses the natural life functions. However, on a perception level, the two etiologies greatly differ.

While in cancer, we have less perception, in schizophrenia we have *more but distorted* perception. The stress is on the less and more.

The distortion is an add-on, but the fact is that the schizophrenic *lives* and the cancer patient is *dead*, even before the symptomatic illness manifests through slowly killing the body; the schizophrenic is creative, while the cancer patient is dull, the schizophrenic is daring while the cancer patient is a bore for himself and his environment.

To state it more bluntly, the schizophrenic is still a *sexual being* while the cancer patient has long ceased to be one.

In a society that venerates impotence and frigidity as something implicitly virtuous and that is afraid of sexuality, it is no wonder that exaggerated social care is taken for the cancer patient and *so much money spent on healing cancer,* while schizophrenics are for the most part left alone, abandoned and despised by the medical health establishment that puts them on an equal level with the criminal! Reich thought that on a perception level, the schizophrenic even surpasses the majority of 'normal' humans:

> Although self perception constitutes self awareness, and although the kind of self perception determines the type of consciousness, these two functions of the mind are not identical. Consciousness appears as a higher function, developed in the organism much later than self perception. Its degree of clarity and oneness depends, to judge from observations in schizophrenic processes, not so much on the strength or intensity of self perception, as on the more or less complete integration of the innumerable elements of self perception into one single experience of the self. (Id., 44)

The higher and more subtle and refined the perception, the more difficult it is for the organism to integrate what is perceived; the more complex a human mind is, the more it borders the schizophrenic process because the *integrating function of the ego* must be stronger than normally so as to prevent a crack-up into sub-personalities that a complex mind encompasses. A Shakespeare, a Blake, a Goethe, and a Beethoven bordered dementia at a much closer distance than *homo normalis*. And a Reich probably as well.

Having a closer look at so-called mental illness, we become quickly aware that most mental diseases are rather *emotional* diseases and that the mental deterioration only comes in later as a consequence of the worsening of the bioenergetic setup of the organism. Reich explains:

> Thus, we must conclude that the mental functions of self perception and consciousness are directly related to, and correspond to, certain bioenergetic states of the organism, in kind as well as in degree. This permits, accordingly, the conclusion that schizophrenia is *a truly biophysical, and not merely a mental, disease.* (Id., 45)

Reich explains this even more clearly, stating that '[e]motions are bioenergetic, plasmatic, and not mental or chemical or mechanical, functions.' (Id.)

Of course, in the old model of a *mechanistic universe* where every phenomenon is seen separately and without connection to other phenomena, either on the same or a higher level of organization, it can hardly be perceived that mental and emotional functions should be inextricably linked.

> It is because psychiatry did not go beyond merely historic thinking and exploration that it bogged down therapeutically. (Id., 48)

Today many people in our culture begin to see the phenomenal world connected in a cosmic structure that is holistically coded and situated on both the microcosmic and the macrocosmic levels. Reich had this perspective decades ago, but was considered by his contemporaries as a crazy mystic; he was really lucid enough to surpass their residual worldview, stating:

> I am referring here to functions which bind man and his cosmic origin into one. In schizophrenia, as well as in true religion and in true art and science, the

awareness of these deep functions is great and overwhelming. (Id., 50)

Reich was against religious indoctrination just as much as Krishnamurti. Yet he knew also what authentic *religio* is; in this original sense of the term, he was religious, was 'linked back' to our origins, our true source. That is why he was able to see the original unity and lucidity behind the distortions of the split psyche:

> In such schizophrenic experiences, the world which is called THE BEYOND in common mysticism and in true religion manifests itself before our eyes. One must learn to read this language. (Id., 60)

Reich's understanding of schizophrenia surpassed the psychiatric standards of his time; and he comes close to our great poets when he writes:

> These great souls, broken down and wrecked as schizophrenic KNOW and PERCEIVE what no homo normalis dares to touch. Let us not be led astray by the distortions of this knowledge. Let us listen to what these gifted and clear visioned human beings have to say. We can learn a great deal from them; we can learn to become more modest, more serious, less gaudy and cocky, and we can start realizing a few of the claims we make in an empty manner in our

churches and in our high academic institutions. I claim, after thirty years of thorough study of schizophrenic minds, that they look through our hypocrisy, our cruelty and stupidity, our fake culture, our evasiveness, and our fear of truth. They had the courage to approach what is commonly evaded, and they were wrecked because they went through the inferno without any help on the part of our neurotic parents, our conceited teachers, our cruel directors of educational institutions, our ignorant physicians. They hoped to emerge from the inferno into the clear, fresh air where only great minds dwell. That they could not make it, that they got stuck in the realm of the devil is not their fault; it is the fault of the abysmal ignorance and stupidity of our homines normales. (Id., 61)

Progressing in Reich's case report, the reader becomes increasingly aware that his initial assumptions were true and sound. In fact, the patient eventually responded positively to the therapy.

The drawbacks were expected to happen from the start and they were perhaps necessary stumble stones or guide posts for the therapist not to lose track of the Ariadne thread, the invisible hand that seemed to guide the whole process.

After one of these crises, Reich, somewhat afflicted, *yet so much the more passionately involved* as a healer, stated:

> Our patient had experienced her emotional storm as great music. The ignoramus will say that's crazy. No, it is not crazy. A Beethoven goes through the same kind of emotional storm when he composes a great symphony, which provides a huge profit for some utterly amusical businessman. It is obvious that a Beethoven has the structure to stand the same kind of great emotional storm that causes the breakdown in the schizophrenic structure. (Id.)

Again, what we usually associate with *dementia* has little in common with the schizophrenic process and is but a symptom, as the cancerous tumor is but a symptom in the greater part of the bioelectric shrinking that cancer represents.

> The emotional and bioenergetic dissociation in the schizophrenic leads, as we well know, sooner or later to a general decay of the organism with bad body odor, loss of weight, severe disturbances of biochemical metabolism, and sometimes also with true cancerous developments. The schizophrenic shrinks biopathically, too, because of the loss of the capacity to take up bioenergy and to maintain its normal level. (Id., 68)

In schizophrenia, we are not only at the borderline between normalcy and genius, but also at the borderline between what we call *rational reality* and *paranormal reality.*

Many of the symptoms that the schizophrenic usually exhibits are, at least in a less distorted or exaggerated form, signs of high intuition or sensitivity, as every paranormal exhibits them.

Since several decades, psychic phenomena are subject to scientific investigation, using controlled and repeatable, verifiable research methods. For example, Uri Geller, the famous psychic, was tested thoroughly during weeks and months at Stanford University for the veracity of his phenomenal psychic powers—and those tests and experiments were so tremendously successful that at present no serious scientist can contest anymore the validity of psychic powers or experiences. That was of course very different at the time when Reich wrote this case report. He states:

> The orgone energy field meter, constructed in 1944 (reference to The Discovery of the Orgone, Vol. II, 1948), demonstrated the existence of an orgone energy field beyond the skin surface of the organism. (Id., 73)

Long before the construction of the *orgone energy field meter* that Reich mentioned, Mesmer construed a similar device in France and other devices are reported by theosophical research and noted in the annals of the *International Society for Psychic Research* in London. Similarly, with regard to a 'sixth sense,' Reich states:

> The existence of the sixth sense, the orgonotic perception beyond the surface of the organism, can, therefore, not be doubted. (Id.)

Modern psychiatry recognizes not only the split personality but equally the borderline personality, allowing a large grey area that surrounds the more and more relativized concept of 'psychiatric normalcy.' However, at Reich's lifetime, this was quite different:

> It is very difficult to formulate in words the experience in which a process in the organism is perceived and yet is not perceived as one's own. But there can be no doubt whatsoever that this is exactly the key to understanding the schizophrenic split and the projection of bodily sensations. (Id., 77)

It might be a key to understanding schizophrenia to see it as a distortion of the natural perception of bodily sensations, and to start the treatment from there. Reich's success in treating the patient *orgonotically* rather than psychologically might be a strong indicator for the *energy approach* being the most effective treatment approach for schizophrenia.

At the end of his report, summarizing the treatment after the thirty-fifth session, Reich was convinced that his initial assumption and his perceptual approach to schizophrenia were true and valid.

> Let us pause for a moment again to think over this situation: the therapeutic result was doubtful as far as restoration of complete sanity was concerned. As a clinical confirmation of the whole theory of organismic orgone biophysics, the situation was invaluable, rich in possibilities, with a broad outlook on the whole realm of human character structure. To sum it up, the following conclusions seemed safe:

> 1. The murderous hate I and my coworkers had met in so many people, laymen and professionals alike, was due to the provocation of spontaneous movements in the body, in bodies which had never experienced such autonomic movements, well-known to every healthy, unarmored individual.

> 2. These movements, if alienated or excluded from the realm of full perception (self-perception),

constitute the experiences of every kind of mysticism. That a psychopath like Hitler preferred to kill in spring thus becomes easily understandable.

3. The influencing forces in schizophrenia are identical with the plasmatic movements in the organism.

4. Many types of crime and murder are due to such sudden changes in the structure of potential or actual murderers.

5. Chronically armored human organisms tolerate only low levels of bioenergy and the corresponding emotions. What constitutes high-pitched joie de vivre in unarmored individuals, their buoyancy, their aliveness, namely the functioning of bioenergy / on a high level with a strong energy metabolism, is utterly unbearable to the armored individual. Sudden changes from a high to a very low energy level constitute acute depression. On the other hand, sudden changes from a chronically low to a very high energy level constitute dramatic and dangerous situations because of the inability to tolerate strong sensations and emotions. (…) It is, therefore, to be expected that biopsychiatry will sooner or later succeed in describing human structures and characteristic reactions in terms of bioenergetic metabolism, emotional tolerance of biophysical excitation, and capacity for energy discharge. Such an energetic point of view would enable us to handle,

finally, human nature, not with complicated ideas
and experiences, but with simple energy functions, as
we are handling the rest of nature. (Id., 79-80)

Having closed the therapy successfully, Reich
reports the patient *completely healed* after a treatment
of almost two years and she wrote him repeatedly
that her mental health was stable and that she was
happily married and had children later on.

Reich's theory reveals the truth of functional
science, of holistic science which is the *energetic view of
all life*, the view that widely prevailed in antiquity
and, until today, in the East. As for schizophrenia,
Reich concludes that the split is actually *not a mental
or psychic phenomenon* in the first place, but the result
of an energy imbalance in the whole of the organism:

> The core of the problem is the biophysical split
> between excitation and perception and the resulting
> intolerance by the biosystem of strong emotions. (Id.,
> 83)

Concluding the therapy, Reich puts his findings in
a universal and phylogenetically important context:

> In this process of mastering the emotional plague, we
> shall encounter homo normalis at his worst; in the
> form of the righteous mystic and of the mechanistic

human animal who run away from themselves for
exactly the same reasons that forced our patient into
the catatonic breakdown: the horror of the plasmatic
currents in an organism which has become incapable
of coping with strong bioenergetic emotions and has
lost the natural function of self-regulation. All attacks
upon our scientific work during the past twenty-five
years have come from such individuals in various
organizations and social bodies. Homo normalis has
fought orgone biophysics for the same reason that
made him burn witches by the thousands, that makes
him shock patients by the millions: the horror of the
life forces in the human animal which is unable to
feel in himself. If we do not muster the courage to
maintain this insight, we shall fail as psychiatrists,
physicians and educators. (Id., 105)

Schizophrenia, seen from this perspective, may
initially be triggered by reject. What comes next is
emotional disturbance. And what is then, much later,
diagnosed as debility or a *shrinking of general vitality* is
again a consequence of the former, a somatization of
it.

Wilhelm Reich's research has the invaluable merit
that it does not only provide effective medical
treatment of schizophrenia, but that it offers all the
tools and insights for understanding the *deeper roots of
schizophrenia* on both an individual and a collective

level. As such it is truly unique and unprecedented in human medical, social and political history.

An Integrative Vision

When asked what is the unique quality of Reich's genius, I would reply that it is his integrative vision. Generally speaking, one insight I gained in my more than thirty years of genius research is that *genius is vision.* It's the ability to see beyond mere appearances and to understand the interconnectedness of all-that-is. I have let the genius talk directly to you, which is why I have provided quotes from a case report he never published and yet that is one of the most fascinating documents about his way of working and at the same time, a document that amply demonstrates the vision he had for the social and political dimensions of his clinical findings. It was this very vision that put off most of his professional colleagues for the reigning paradigm in science and medical care was mechanistic; hence, most of these remarks would have been considered off-track, useless or even nonsensical. In addition, the *Reich-Einstein Affair* seems to indicate that an undoubted genius, his contemporary, Albert Einstein, was unaware of Reich's cognitive abilities and professional skills; this is quite astonishing given that Einstein habitually possessed sound judgment regarding other remarkable people.

In my opinion—this is the only way I can explain this strange affair—Einstein was not objective in Reich's case; he was probably influenced against Reich, which is, given the scandalous propaganda against Reich's extraordinary discoveries, nothing to wonder about.

The best way to describe what I mean by an *integrative vision* is to once again refer to Leonardo, whose multivectorial genius is undisputed. In the words of Fritjof Capra, Leonardo's vision was always encompassing the hidden connections between apparently unrelated phenomena in science and art.

The Schizophrenic Split (1945) shows in a perhaps most convincing manner how Reich saw the interconnectedness between personal and collective schizophrenia; while he was compassionate regarding the suffering of an individual who has been declared as 'crazy' by the mental health establishment, he was boldly scandalized about the schizoid split in the whole of our society, the internal crack-up our society seems to suffer from as a result of large-scale hypocrisy and the repression of our primary emotions.

Chapter Three
The Genius of Albert Einstein

We do not really know if Leonardo or Reich were child prodigies. In Reich's case, all points to the contrary. However, we know that Einstein's wit was manifesting early, and that he was premature in his psychosexual development. At the age of fourteen he had a level of autonomy that is seldom to be found with modern consumer children.

 Einstein's Jewish upbringing may also have contributed to his early maturity. It is known that Germanic non-orthodox Jews raise their children without harsh punishments, in a trusting manner; they concede their offspring a considerable margin of personal movement, and talk to them as one would talk to an adult.

Einstein was not the man interested in making the world talk about him. He was gifted with that sense of humility that I have seen with other people I believe have or had genius in what they do or did. I have seen this humility with Alexander Lowen, with Fritjof Capra and with Françoise Dolto—and we know it equally from Picasso. I have also come to understand over the years that most people in our modern world have a quite opposite character in that after their comparatively modest successes they usually become willful and arrogant, blocking their email addresses, and thinking of themselves as 'beyond reach,' remaining in touch only with a chosen few. These people seem to ignore the old adage that says, 'there is no greater enemy to large-scale success than petty little success.'

And perhaps not astonishingly so, I have seen over and over in my life that geniuses start not from a smooth lift that is given to them by the kind help of others, but to the contrary, by adverse circumstances. Both Wilhelm Reich and Françoise Dolto suffered the fate to being excluded from the *International Psychoanalytic Association* when they were developing the first crucial outbursts of their later ground-breaking theories.

Leonardo, at the very start of his professional life, in 1476, was charged with sodomy but was fortunately acquitted, as homosexuality, at that time was still a capital crime.

Picasso suffered years of the most pitiful poverty when living as a young painter in Paris, sometimes being forced to sell paintings for a meal or firing them up in the chimney for not freezing to death in the winters. Glenn Gould was laughed in the face by musical critics and even the great public before his breakthrough with the *Goldberg Variations* in 1955, as his mannerism was contrary to 'good taste' at the time. Svjatoslav Richter passed years behind the iron curtain, becoming a living myth in the West, until his début at Carnegie Hall in 1960, when Richter was already 45 years old.

Einstein's life, as recounted in some biographies, comes over as the tranquil existence of an absent-minded and good-tempered elder who was just lucky enough to be 'so smart,' and who 'certainly got all the help he needed to succeed.'

Nothing could be further from the truth. Einstein struggled with major engagements all his life, for all kinds of humanitarian causes, the Jewish cause being just one of them, and he was not at all leading a tranquil life. To begin with, he had to flee the Nazis, and contrary to other Jews he was lucid enough to see coming what was coming, and he took flight already in 1932, a good year before Hitler came to power in Germany. It was his keen sense of political reality that saved him from further trouble here, but it also has to be seen that he had a polite and non-obtrusive behavior, once living in the country that received him well, the United States of America.

And here he shows a similar behavior pattern with other highly gifted Jews who, for similar reasons, fled their home countries, such as Arthur Rubinstein,

Sergei Rachmaninov, Vladimir Horowitz, to name only these, and who had a similarly smooth character toward the authorities which allowed them to really enjoy their expatriate lives.

It also has to be seen in this picture of 'tranquility' and secure fame that the FBI had conducted an investigation against Einstein because of his affiliations with *Zionism, Communism* and *Socialism*, which resulted in an almost 1500 pages dossier, which is by now declassified.

Einstein was not doing very well in school, while he generally got along above average, but he did not enjoy his *Lehrjahre*, to use the wording of the poet Jean Paul. He was glad to have found the job in the patent office in Berne, after two years of fruitless job search and a more than inconsistent university career, and married his first wife hurriedly, in that bachelor situation, probably for the reason of pregnancy.

That marriage may have given a sense of stability to his life, which may in turn have contributed to his incredible vigor that made him achieve his first major papers in a situation at work, where he was a full-time government employee, and at home, with a small baby around.

Then, one must seriously ponder his letters to President Roosevelt dated August 2, 1939 that led, on a purely causal line of reasoning, to the destruction of Hiroshima and Nagasaki.

While it was of course virtuous to warn about Hitler, intuiting that Hitler was developing a technology that as we know today was set to produce mass destruction weapons, fact was that the Roosevelt administration did not imply him in any way in the development and testing of atomic weapons, and that he had thus no control over the spark he had given to a gigantic barrel of dynamite.

He had written in the first letter that America should put their own hand on nuclear research, and stated that he felt that it would be possible to build 'extremely powerful bombs of a new type.' When one considers this single sentence written from a man who called himself, in his own words, 'not only a pacifist but a militant pacifist,' one who is 'willing to fight for peace,' one wonders how the construction of 'powerful bombs of a new type' would ever bring humanity closer to peace?

 How could a man of the intelligence of Einstein commit such a lapse in his logical thinking ability? He knew more about the power of the Hitler government than ordinary people; he possessed information that many didn't have, and that today we all know, but that was simply not available to ordinary American citizens at the time.

Hitler was not taken for what he was, by the Roosevelt administration, which is one of the reasons why the United States entered the war so late, and why Hitler's power and strategy for world dominion was constantly belittled. Even Churchill had a hard time to convince the British government and military to take action against Hitler, and much damage was done to Britain because of that underestimation of their enemy. Einstein was probably sincerely worried that Hitler might achieve all his demonic goals and he might have felt it was his sincere duty as an American citizen to prevent the worst. Newer research on the Nazi regime suggests that Einstein's estimations were not far-fetched and that Hitler's nuclear and antigravity research was by far more advanced than British or American weaponry experts had assumed it at the time.

Einstein suggested President Roosevelt in the first letter that 'in view of the situation you may think it desirable to have more permanent contact maintained between the Administration and the group of physicists working on chain reactions in America;' yet the government did that research single-handedly and under the seal of top secrecy.

Albert Einstein
Old Grove Rd.
Nassau Point
Peconic, Long Island

August 2nd, 1939

F.D. Roosevelt,
President of the United States,
White House
Washington, D.C.

Sir:

Some recent work by E.Fermi and L. Szilard, which has been communicated to me in manuscript, leads me to expect that the element uranium may be turned into a new and important source of energy in the immediate future. Certain aspects of the situation which has arisen seem to call for watchfulness and, if necessary, quick action on the part of the Administration. I believe therefore that it is my duty to bring to your attention the following facts and recommendations:

In the course of the last four months it has been made probable - through the work of Joliot in France as well as Fermi and Szilard in America - that it may become possible to set up a nuclear chain reaction in a large mass of uranium,by which vast amounts of power and large quantities of new radium-like elements would be generated. Now it appears almost certain that this could be achieved in the immediate future.

This new phenomenon would also lead to the construction of bombs, and it is conceivable - though much less certain - that extremely powerful bombs of a new type may thus be constructed. A single bomb of this type, carried by boat and exploded in a port, might very well destroy the whole port together with some of the surrounding territory. However, such bombs might very well prove to be too heavy for transportation by air.

Roosevelt well replied to Einstein's first letter and set in place a committee for that purpose but subsequently things did not develop in the sense Einstein expected.

While in the second letter, dated March 7, 1940, Einstein gives Roosevelt detailed information about uranium research in Germany, and while from the third letter, equally from 1940, there is only a fragment left, the fourth letter, dated March 25, 1945, gives a conclusive answer.

—See Ronald Clarke, Einstein: The Life and Times, New York: Avon Books, 1971, 678-679, and 681.

It namely becomes evident that the driving force behind the whole event was the Hungarian physicist Dr. L. Szilard, who is known to have developed the atomic chain reaction. This is suggested by researchers also because of the fact that the first letter was dispatched under Szilard's address in Long Island, not Einstein's in Princeton; biographers even assume that Szilard himself drafted the letters and Einstein just signed them and sent them under his name.

In the fourth letter, Einstein reveals that the incentive for his first letter, back in 1939, had been originating from Dr. Szilard, whom he cites as 'one of the discoverers of the neutron emission of uranium.' He then writes that the terms of secrecy under which Dr. Szilard was working did not permit him to give information about his work, and he stresses that Szilard 'is now greatly concerned about the lack of adequate contact between scientist[s] who are doing this work and those members of your Cabinet who are responsible for formulating policy.'

In other words, Szilard was not sure what was going on, from 1939 to 1945, over six long years. He had been put on ice, and the research was conducted by the military without interacting with scientists.

—See William Lanouette, Bela Silard, Genius in the Shadows: A Biography of Leo Szilard, Chicago: Chicago University Press, 1994, 261-262.

The letter however did not reach Roosevelt before his death on April 12, 1945. Richard Rhodes writes in his book *The Making of the Atomic Bomb (1995)* that even before the first test detonation, many scientists and military communities were already expressing moral misgivings about the creation of a device that was *just ten feet long with a payload yield equivalent to twenty thousand tons of high explosives.* And of course, Einstein and nobody else foresaw the sudden death of

Franklin D. Roosevelt during the famous *Unfinished Portrait* session. Harry Truman and Winston Churchill then issued an ultimatum against Japan, known as the 'Potsdam Declaration,' which warned Japan to make a complete and unconditional surrender or risk 'prompt and utter destruction.' The bomb itself was of course not mentioned directly and this vague caveat was all the Japanese received in a way of a warning.

On August 6, 1945, the nuclear bomb 'Little Boy' was dropped on Hiroshima, Japan, by an American bomber, directly killing an estimated eighty thousand people; by the end of the year, injury and radiation brought total casualties to up until one hundred forty thousand victims. Almost 70% of the city was destroyed. On August 9, 1945, a second atomic bomb nicknamed 'Fat Man' was dropped on Nagasaki, Japan, which caused the immediate death of forty thousand people, but because of the nuclear after-effects, it was effectively a number of almost eighty thousand that was suffering ill-health and death through this catastrophe. The atomic mushroom cloud from the explosion that hovered over Nagasaki was rising sixty thousand feet into the air on the morning of that day.

We know that Einstein later took full responsibility for the letter issue, calling it 'the single greatest mistake' of his life. I think one must put oneself in his skin to really become aware of what that means. Another would perhaps have committed suicide. Only a person of virtue and true humility could live to old age with such a karmic debt; for that Einstein has triggered a *karmic entanglement*, and thus bears a participatory responsibility for the catastrophe as a result of his deliberate involvement in that matter cannot be doubted.

However, it must also be seen that it was all but certain in 1939 and 1940 that Hitler would be ultimately defeated, for at that time, Hitler was close to final victory at some point between 1942 and 1945, and the decisive parameters of the conflict were changing just only over the course of the last months before the final defeat of Germany in the war.

Einstein is known to have said to Linus Pauling, in 1954, 'when I signed the letter to President Roosevelt recommending that atom bombs be made, (…) there was some justification—the danger that the Germans would make them.'

—Ronald Clarke, Einstein: The Life and Times (1971), 620.

In fact, an evaluation of newest research on the antigravity weapons the Nazis developed at that time secretly under a very competent pulpit, namely the later NASA expert Wernher von Braun, we can say that Einstein's fear was not too far-fetched.

—See, for example, Paul A. LaViolette, Secrets of Antigravity Propulsion: Tesla, UFOs, and Classified Aerospace Technology, New York: Bear & Company, 2008 and The U.S. Antigravity Squadron, in: Thomas Valone, Ed., Electrogravitics Systems: Reports on a New Propulsion Methodology, Washington, D.C.: Integrity Research Institute, 1993, 78-96. See also Tsuyoshi Hasegawa, Racing the Enemy: Stalin, Truman, and the Surrender of Japan, Cambridge, MA: Belknap Press of Harvard University, 2006.

On the other hand, when a declared 'militant pacifist' uses his militarism to initiate and actively support the development of mass destruction weapons—whoever ultimately is going to be the target of those weapons—then one must wonder what *pacifism* actually means?

In addition, it has to be seen that a *clear deliberate involvement* of scientists in high-level politics is unusual, at all times, while we got a glimpse of it with Leonardo who made a substantial part of his living construing weapons for princes and barons.

I feel that a definite answer to this hairy question is hard to give; what we can do is to concede Einstein that he was a human *before* being a genius—with all that that implies!

Chapter Four

The Genius of Svjatoslav Richter

His personality was greater than the possibilities offered to him by the piano, broader than the very concept of complete mastery of the instrument.

—Pierre Boulez

Some Autobiographical Notes

My interest in *Svjatoslav Richter (1915-1997)* rose up the very year of my entering law school, 1975. It was that year, when I was twenty years old, that marked my deep marriage with music for the decades to come. In these early years, coinciding with my late starting of piano performance, meeting with Richter's immense repertoire was a deeply moving and ultimately transformative experience.

From 1975 to 1982, I acquired, from the little money I had left at the time, the whole of the available Richter performances on vinyl record. There was a number of them, however, that were sold out not only in Germany and France, but that I could not even order with a wholesale dealer in California where I had surprisingly found a few that had been sold out since long in Europe. In the summer of 1982, I contacted Richter's concert agent in Munich, Mr. Metaxas, telling him I wanted to give a letter to Maestro Richter, and he pointed me to a recital in Paris, the upcoming month.

In the letter, I was telling Richter of the sad state of affairs regarding the collections of his records available in Germany, France and the United States. Then I went to Paris and attended his Szymanowski recital, yet was unable to meet him as he went to the hotel right after each of the two concerts. Eventually, I talked to Nina Dorliac, his partner, and handed her the letter. She promised me a reply which I never received, yet to my great astonishment, one after one of the sold-out recordings that I had listed in the letter were republished over the coming years.

At that time, I was taking piano lessons with Alexander Sellier, a professor at Saarland Music

Conservatory in Saarbrücken, who was a student of Walter Gieseking, Wilhelm Backhaus and Edwin Fischer, a regionally famed pianist. But he was playing only a tiny part of the piano repertoire, mostly Mozart and Beethoven, and did not at all appreciate my interest in Russian and French composers. Actually he simply could not play them.

In addition, he lost the score of a piano etude I had composed and given to him for evaluation, and of which I had not made a copy. I took this as the main reason for stopping the rather expensive private lessons with him and continued on my own, simply listening to Richter's recordings over and over, every day for at least two hours, and slowly, I began to understand what makes the brick and mortar of great musical performance and authentic rendering of musical masterworks.

It turned out I could not possibly have found a better piano teacher, and my progress was astounding everybody around. Nothing but listening to Richter was the best teaching I could ever have found. Please note that at that time, there was no Internet yet, and Richter was almost never featured on German radio and television, so I had the records alone.

Genius Research Applied

When I started my genius research at that same time, I began to reflect about what it was that made Richter so different from other pianists of that time, and generally, of all times? I began to wonder how his unique genius of musical performance could be put in words?

I noticed that Richter's genius was not just musical performance in the strict sense of the word. It is noteworthy to remind the conversation Richter had in Tokyo with the director of a piano house that is featured in Monsaingeon's movie, and where, upon the amused remark that it was notorious that 'Maestro Richter does not seem to like pianos very much,' he replied that indeed he liked *music* more, and upon the witty reply that Maestro Richter seems to not like pianists very much either, he replied, he in fact liked *musicians* more. These little funny interjections must be understood right in context so that the reader may see their significance, for, to be true, they were *not* meant as jokes!

—Bruno Monsaingeon, Svjatoslav Richter: Notebooks and Conversations, Princeton: Princeton University Press, 2002 and Richter – The Enigma / L'Insoumis / Der Unbeugsame, NVC Arts 1998 (DVD)

There is more than a grain of truth in the rumors about Richter the piano house director mentioned. Richter has been reproached often in his musical career that he didn't care about the quality of pianos he performed on, and this is true, he *really did not care.* He had fostered, as he voiced it in the movie, the magic belief that once he worried about those peripheral issues, those concerns could sidetrack him from his strong focus on the music he was going to interpret.

It is also true that Richter did not think high of most pianists, except very few noted pianists of the time such as for example, Arthur Rubinstein or Glenn Gould; in fact, most of his friends were art dealers, painters, cinematographers, poets, and high-rank composers such as Shostakovich, Prokofiev, and Britten. His visits to Arthur Rubinstein and Vladimir Horowitz in New York City, during his US tour, as they are featured in the movie, were formal and rather pointed events, while Richter had no enduring friendship with any of these and other great pianists of the time. In fact, in Richter's *Notebooks,* many biting remarks can be found about a number of pianists and their way to slop over details in musical scores, and a famous and very talented musician is among them,

Glenn Gould. He seemed to be angered that Gould did not obey Bach's repetition marks in the *Goldberg Variations*, while Gould was a great fan of Richter.

Fact is that Richter did not head toward a pianistic career at all. He wanted to become a painter during his adolescence, and was a painter actually all through his life, and his paintings were often shown in exhibitions in Russia, France and later also in the United States and Australia. It is important to retain this detail here, for it is essential for understanding Richter's genius, which was more than just musical. When Richter started to work at the Odessa Opera as a repetitor, at the age of fifteen, his motivation was primarily to make some money and get on his own feet. For it has to be seen that just a year before, Richter's father was killed by Russian nationalists in

Odessa, who mistook him for a 'German spy,' and Richter might have wanted to contribute to the household income.

Richter did not see a career perspective yet in the musical domain. He was not yet sure of himself at that time; after all he was still a youngster. That was in 1930. Four years later, Richter gave his first recital to a greater audience in a business club in Odessa, while he has given many small recitals within the larger family, and as a child already for peers, but those were not meeting the expectations of his father, a German pianist. Richter's mother, however, from a noble Russian family, insisted that no strict guidance should be imposed upon Svjatoslav; his mother in fact trusted her son's innate genius.

Multiple Talents, One Decision, One Career

But these events are rather insignificant because they were not yet based upon a *decision*. Richter was not clear about his mission and his life's work until he took the somewhat surprising decision to take formal piano lessons with Heinrich Neuhaus in Moscow. It has to be seen that in the normal course of events the pianists that teachers of his rank accept for their master classes have gone through a full-cycle pianistic education. Richter had done nothing of that.

—Heinrich Neuhaus, The Art of Piano Playing, London: Barrie & Jenkins, 1973, first published in 1958.

He had played in night clubs and accompanied fanciful opera singers in what was considered, at the time, a 'provincial' town. While Neuhaus accepted him, immediately sensing his genius, Richter's pianistic career was all but taken for granted. Despite the fact that his intellectual, musical and manual capacities were enormous, Richter's fate was not an easy one. He was meeting with lots of indifference, even reject in his early years. He goes over all that in a light mood in Monsaingeon's movie, but we must put

ourselves in his skin for a moment to feel the hurt and
frustration he suffered for more of a decade of his
career. Audiences were reacting with estrangement,
because Richter's play was markedly different from
all they had heard before.

In Prague, for example, where later he was adored
like a god, he first encountered blatant reject and
ridicule. In London, in 1961, despite his brilliant
Carnegie Hall début just a year before, he really faced
a hostile reaction from British critics until his
memorable performance of the Liszt concertos later
that year.

When fame hit Richter, it hit him strongly, totally,
and virtually until his leaving the earth plane. While
he ended his life with a short period of reduced
memory and sight, and suffered from a nasty
distortion of his musical pitch, he was productive all
through his life cycle. More importantly, it is
significant to see how focused he was once he had
made his choice. Charles Munch, Eugene Ormandy,
Pierre Boulez, to name only these, from his closer
circle of friends, tried repeatedly to get him into
conducting, but he is said to have resigned with the
statement: 'I do not like three things, analysis, power,
and conducting.'

But of course, from a career consultant's point of view, Richter was right on spot, as when there is no real need to change one's main orientation, *one should not do so,* as this will lead to energy dissipation and a confusion of one's main audience. Richter did it right.

No Prodigal Son, and No Prodigy

In an interview with Johannes Schaaf, a German filmmaker, in the 1970s, which I watched on German television, Richter explained he had benefited from his parents never forcing him to practice the piano, giving him freedom for the gradual unfolding of his talents and interests. This had built in him the doggedness, and self-confidence to endure those first years until he was finally, and very gradually, recognized.

 It is important to understand that Richter's career was fundamentally different from the careers of child prodigies, as for example Mozart, Mendelssohn, Liszt, Ravel or Arrau, for various reasons. Richter, contrary to musical child prodigies, was *not* a musical genius only, but rather on the line of

multivectorial geniuses like Leonardo, or Einstein, which is after all the reason why I included him in this book.

Richter was not only a musician, but also a poet, a painter, a philosopher, and, while this is never mentioned anywhere, an *actor*. He was stunningly honest in the interviews with Bruno Monsaingeon, telling the audience that what he basically learnt from Neuhaus was 'presenting himself in a theatrical manner,' posing in a way to attract the attention of the audience before he ever played the first note of the recital. These remarks were not said in a joking manner, but Richter, who was naturally a rather shy and remote person, obviously needed this boost of his self-confidence to fully realize his genius in musical performance.

Some Details of Richter's Genius

Now, coming to the essential, I shall give some detail to my claim that Richter was an unheard-of musical genius, and perhaps the best pianist of the 20th century. First of all, let me say that Richter's genius was such that it can't be described with just listing a few qualities of his play, as this can be done with every good and talented musician. There is much more, and there is a level of complexity in it all that I haven't encountered with any other musician I know and have studied.

Before I go more in detail, I would like to shortly outline the main characteristics that describe Richter's musical and pianistic genius. I will then try to explain every single characteristic and give at least one musical example.

I would list these elements as follows, while this list is non-exhaustive:

▸ Innate and intuitive *musical perception* and accordingly, an extraordinary *accuracy of style*, uniqueness and cultural imbeddedness of a musical composition;

▸ An almost magical *correctness of taste*, which gives to each composition rendered a feel of *striking authenticity and originality*, whereby observing the composer's intention in most meticulous detail;

▸ The perception of a musical piece in *whole patterns*, not single notes or measures, that is, in larger comprehensively linked units that makes that the listener perceives the musical structure 'from a bird perspective;'

▸ A *musical intelligence* that with astounding clarity discards out lesser original compositions, focusing only on masterworks, combined with a *strict eclecticism* which can serve as a guide for the music student, and wide audiences;

- The ability to play a wide range of chamber music without previous in-depth study of the piano score, with a *perfect sight-reading ability* that was so accurate as to the slightest details that it has dumbfounded musicians and lay people alike;

- The ability to play *large musical compositions*, such as whole operas or symphonies, from the conductor's score, whereby transposing the keys for the various instruments in real time, and transcribing the whole complex structure for the piano, while playing it;

- An astounding *natural sense for rhythm* that was so accurate that critics spoke about Richter's feeling of 'time' especially when he performed Baroque music; contrary to many other pianists, he has never been found to accelerate a piece unduly, or to slow it down through *rubati*, except such was written in the score;

- One of the *largest musical memories known in the entire history of musical performance*, enabling him at the peak of his career to play about eighty entire musical programs, or roughly 160 hours of uninterrupted music from memory;

- A faculty of concentration so high, combined with a physical endurance so great that he was able to practice *ten to twelve hours for a recital*, and then, in the evening, did the recital, without a moment of sleep in between;

- The ability to be *undisturbed* by even major noise, turmoil or shortcomings during a recital, enduring it stoically, while continuing to play, rendering his best performances not in the studio but in live recitals, which is why most of his recordings are live cuts from recitals, and only exceptionally, studio recordings;

- Fate has given Richter the best of the best in terms of physical constitution. He had hands so large as before him only Anton Rubinstein, Ferruccio Busoni and

Sergei Rachmaninov, able to grasp a twelfth; large hands alone, however, do not make a great pianist. Richter had an unbelievable speed in wrist positioning combined with an accurate, never-failing safety for underarm transport, that is ultimately facilitated by strong and relaxed shoulder and spine muscles;

▸ Richter had what I only can call a 'Shakespearean' appearance, which came from his natural attraction to acting and theater; this talent was hardly ever mentioned in any of his various biographies, but it was obvious to me when I saw him playing Szymanowski in the *Salle Gaveau* in Paris, back in 1982.

INNATE AND INTUITIVE MUSICAL PERCEPTION

To begin with, I was positively intrigued when reading in Neuhaus' book *The Art of Piano Playing (1958/1973)* that my view about Richter's genius coincided with what Neuhaus, his teacher, had thought about him. It was among other details the fact that Richter had a faculty of conception of a musical composition that I would call 'immediate, total and holistic.' It did not surprise me to read in that book that questions of *musical perception or taste* had never been a subject in the teaching relation Neuhaus-Richter, simply because Richter's perception of a musical piece was innate and so absolute and to a point one could only agree or disagree. But the matter is more complex, as Richter not only grasped with a never-failing intuition the musical piece in its absoluteness, in its uniqueness, but he also embedded it in a space of culture where it belongs because its composer lived in a certain time and space that is defined by musical history.

CORRECTNESS OF TASTE

And here is where taste comes in. What is taste? It's not really something that can't be measured. Richter relates in *Richter the Enigma* that Maria Yudina, shortly after Russia's entering World War II, played a Prelude from Bach's *Well-Tempered Clavier* in a public performance like a war march, and upon Richter's question after the concert why she did that, she replied, almost angry about the question:

—But we are at war!

Richter recounts that with a sense of humor, but it was not with humor that Yudina, on her part, related to the public she thought that Richter was 'a Rachmaninov pianist.'

This was not taken as a compliment by Richter, but as an insult, and it must be one for a performer who has covered almost the entire piano repertoire, including all musical styles that ever were used for composing piano music.

Richter had a sense of taste so correct, so adequate for each and every musical style and epoch that I consider him unique with this faculty in the whole of musical performance history.

For example, many pianists, when they play Schubert, make his music sound like a smaller Beethoven, instead of a fully grown Schubert, or they play Rachmaninov as if it was a somewhat 'russianized' vintage of Chopin. To have a sense of taste means that one is able to let the music sound 'authentic,' which is a very complex task.

To accomplish this task, it's surely not enough to be a pianist alone, to have a good piano technique, or to be able to master technical difficulties. It is required that one be a musician, an artist, a poet, and a philosopher to understand this level of complexity.

That means one must realize a consistent approach for not just a single piano piece, but with an intention for rendering *a whole composer*, with all of his or her oeuvres consistently and authentically. I do not know any pianist over the whole of musical history who had this faculty, except Richter. And the composers themselves are for obvious reasons the least gifted for rendering the works of other composers. When you hear how Rachmaninov played a Chopin Scherzo and you heard Richter play Chopin's *Scherzi*, you will stop listening to Rachmaninov's interpretation, except for reasons of musical and autobiographical research.

PERCEPTION OF WHOLE PATTERNS

Every piece Richter plays, even if he plays it slower than other pianists, seems to be faster to the listener, subjectively, because Richter lets us see the piece as if from a 'bird perspective,' so that the single detail is imbedded in all its beauty in a greater unit, like a *pattern*, or movement.

This becomes especially obvious with Sonatas, where Richter, contrary to many pianists, always plays *all the repetitions*, and yet, one doesn't feel bored a single moment. In the contrary, the repetitions become organic when Richter plays them, and one feels that there is a logic in repeating a part.

Glenn Gould, who, interestingly enough, is one of the pianists who most often skipped repetitions, even in his famous rendition of Bach's *Goldberg Variations*, relates in *Richter the Enigma (1998):*

> I always believed that it's possible to divide musical performers into two categories, those who seek to exploit the instrument they use, and those who do

not. In the first category, if we believe the history books, one can find a place for such legendary characters as Liszt and Paganini, as well as any number of allegedly demonic virtuosi of more recent vintage. That category belongs essentially to musicians who are determined to make us aware of their relationship with their instrument, whatever it happens to be. They allow that relationship to become the focus of attention. The second category, on the other hand, includes musicians who try to bypass the whole question of performing mechanism, to create the illusion of a direct link between themselves and the particular musical score, and therefore help the listener to achieve a sense of involvement, not the with the performance per se but rather with the music itself. And I think that in our time there is no better example of that second kind of musician than Svjatoslav Richter.

What Svjatoslav Richter does in fact is insert between the listener and the composer his own enormously powerful personality, as a kind of conduit, and as he does this, we gain the impression that we're discovering the work anew and, often, from a quite different perspective than that to which we were accustomed.

The first time I heard him play was at the Moscow Conservatory, in May 1957, and he opened his program with the last of Schubert's sonatas, the Sonata in B Flat Major. It's a very long sonata, one of the longest ever written, in fact, and Richter played it at what I believe to be the slowest tempo I've ever heard, thereby making it a good deal longer, needless to say. I think, at this point, it's appropriate to confess two things. The first is that, heretical though it may be, I'm not really addicted to most of Schubert's music. I find myself usually unable to come to terms with the repetitive structures involved, and I find that I get very restless and squirmy already when I have to sit through one of the longer Schubert essays. Well, what happened in fact was that, for the next hour I was in a state that I can only compare to a hypnotic trance.

All of my prejudices about Schubert's repetitive structures were forgotten; musical details which I'd previously considered to be ornamental were given the appearance of organic elements. In fact I can remember many of those details to this day. And it seemed to me that I was witnessing a union of two supposedly irreconcilable qualities, intense analytical calculation revealed through a spontaneity equivalent to improvisation. And I realized at that moment, as I have on many subsequent occasions when I have been listening to Richter's recordings, that I was in the presence of one of the most powerful communicators the world of music has produced in our time.

MUSICAL INTELLIGENCE AND ECLECTICISM

Richter has been a guide to me, in the whole of my musical development. I simply followed his selective instinct for the music I wanted to play. In every case when I was in doubt why he didn't play other pieces of one same collection, I listened to those pieces rendered by other pianists—and was regularly disappointed!

I would have wasted my time had I practiced any of them. On the other hand, Richter played music that was forgotten or that was not popular at his time, thereby rendering a great service to many a composer, even a genius such as Prokofiev. For example, Richter relates in *Richter the Enigma* that Prokofiev's 5th Piano Concerto had never been a big public success, which is why Prokofiev asked Richter to perform it, and the performance was a resounding success. Heinrich Neuhaus relates in *The Art of Piano Playing (1958/1973)*:

> Richter does not confine himself to playing Soviet, Russian and Western classical music, but he repeatedly performs in various cities of the USSR the whole of Bach's *Wohltemperiertes Klavier* (apart from other Bach compositions). He has literally brought back to life the marvelous Schubert sonatas and some Weber sonatas that for some reason had been forgotten, and has played a multitude of seldom heard pieces by Liszt, Schumann, Beethoven; in short his concerts not only give pleasure to a wide audience but also open before it new horizons and bring before

it excellent little-known compositions, thus constantly broadening and raising the level of artistic culture and musical experience. (Id., 204)

IMPECCABLE SIGHT-READING CAPABILITY

With regard to performing chamber music, I have often observed that even manually lesser gifted pianists are able to accompany singers or play a part in a chamber orchestra simply because they are excellent sight readers. Heinrich Neuhaus relates in *The Art of Piano Playing (1958/1973)* about Richter's sight-reading capabilities:

> When sight-reading a piece for the first time— whether a piano composition, an opera, a symphony, anything—he [Richter] immediately gives an almost perfect rendering, both from the point of view of content and from the point of view of technical skill (in this case, one and the same thing). (Id., 8)

THE ABILITY TO PLAY COMPLEX SCORES

The ability to play an orchestral score on the piano, while on the spot transposing the voices for the two hands is a skill taught in conductor's classes, not a skill that pianists usually possess or practice. The pianist usually plays a score that is set for the two hands, with the upper row representing the right-hand part, and the lower row, the left-hand part.

That means that if a pianist is not able to play an orchestral score at sight, he would have to rewrite it, note for note, on a new set of sheets, transposing all the voices accordingly. This is a work usually done by musical arrangers, who are professionals in their own right, and who are seldom good pianists.

Now, after this short introduction, the reader may get an idea how incredibly complex it must be to do this transcription in real-time. This is still more complex when, as in Richter's case, the score is not just a symphony, but an opera, where the pianist has to let one musical line 'sing' as if it was standing above all the others. There is about nothing in the whole of musical performance that is as complex, difficult and monumental as playing whole operas on the piano, as Richter did in his younger years, when he performed the entire Wagner on the piano in the Musical Academy in Moscow.

NATURAL SENSE FOR RHYTHM

Richter's sense of rhythm is so accurate and so natural that it gives a sense of magic to each and every musical piece he performs. There are many striking examples in the whole of his discography, and I may just mention a couple of them here.

The first example that comes to mind is Richter's famous rendering of Schubert's *Wanderer Fantasie* that is so unique, so monumental, so dramatic and so accurate that it has been acclaimed to be the best rendering of this musical piece in the whole of musical performance history.

I fully agree. Among the many qualities that Richter's play shows in this difficult-to-play, long and complicated piece, his sense for the rhythmic structure of the composition is perhaps the most striking. The pulse is set with the first tempestuous measures that are like a sweeping storm set in music, but subsequently this pulse is variated and modified throughout the piece, and at each transformation, Richter is able to set a new pulse that however is related to the former in a way that the whole is more than an assembly of its parts, and comes over as *intrinsically organic, natural and powerful.*

The second example is Bach's D Minor Prelude from the 1st Volume of Bach's *Well-Tempered Clavier* (BWV 851), which in Richter's rendering gets an expression of eternity and a quality of 'ultimate-truth' through the flow of the triplets in the right hand against the simple eights in the left. I played this piece many times and found out that this magical 'flow character' comes about only when you are able to keep the rhythm with ultimate precision without however being stiff about it because then, it would sound mechanical.

The third example is how Richter plays the *Allegro* from the *Second Handel Suite* in F Major. He plays this piece faster than all the recordings I know of, but with an incredible precision of rhythm and musical detail, and here, of course, his large hands helped him to master some difficulties that come up when you play it that fast. But Richter's rendering gives to that piece a sense of humor and a boyscoutish vitality that is almost hilarious, but anyway uplifting and spirited.

The magic here is the combination of speed with masterful handling of the rhythm. What happens to most pianists is that the faster they play, the more they tend to 'run away' with the piece, which destroys the rhythmic flow.

MUSICAL MEMORY

I have already given an idea of Richter's colossal repertoire and his astounding memory. It should be noted here that memory decreases with age and this was true in Richter's case as well, which may be one of the reasons why later in life, he used to play with the score. However, in all the best years of his career, Richter's memory was simply gigantic, and what's perhaps noteworthy is that it was not just his memory for music, but in general, for all details in life. In *Richter the Enigma*, Richter reveals with a sense of humor that he even remembers the complicated Russian names of all the eight 'strange birds' (old-fashioned virgin sisters) for whom he had played when he was a boy. He also remembered the precise day and year of that performance, and where it was, how the house was looking like, what kind of furniture was around, what had been on every table, what color the tablecloth had, and so on and so forth. He also revealed in that interview that he had suffered much in his life through the fact that he simply could not forget anything, even if he wanted to.

FACULTY OF CONCENTRATION & PHYSICAL ENDURANCE

It is noteworthy that Richter always lived a very simple life, with regular walks in nature, preferably in forests, that he was a very strongly built man, and that he did not spoil his fitness through a 'luxury' lifestyle as so many other pianists, among them, the perhaps most notorious example, Franz Liszt. It has been written often that Richter had an unusual faculty of concentration and physical endurance, and as this is almost general knowledge, I would like to give just two examples here. When he rehearsed Schubert's *Wanderer Fantasie*, he was not sure which piano he preferred, as he had both a Steinway and a Bösendorfer at his disposition. Early in the morning, at the start of the recording session, Richter decided for the Steinway and recorded the whole fantasy. But at the end of the afternoon, when the technicians were about to leave the studio, Richter was suddenly skeptical as to the Steinway being the right piano for this music, and decided for the Bösendorfer. Thus, he continued rehearsing and played the whole piece once again on the Bösendorfer, until late in the night.

The other example is my own meeting with Richter and Nina Dorliac in Paris, which revealed that Richter had rehearsed entire *12 hours* before the recital, as Dorliac told me. It it noteworthy that in the movie, Richter defended the view that he did not practice more than about three hours per day, but Dorliac contradicted this allegation vehemently. At any rate, if he wanted to, he could do it, he was physically able to do marathons of that kind.

THE ABILITY TO BE UNDISTURBED

Richter relates in the movie that during Stalin's funeral, when he was in midst of his recital, once of a sudden the military orchestra was starting to play, but that he went on playing undisturbed, while being scandalized that such had been done to his art! In addition, Richter notes with a sense of humor in the interview that during his younger years, he often had to play in the war, when bombs were falling all around in the city, but that that had never really disturbed him. In all of Richter's recordings from Russia, probably because of the rough climate, there is an almost unbearable background noise of people coughing in all possible ways. Richter never showed the slightest disturbance about that.

PHYSICAL CONSTITUTION AND SIZE OF HANDS

Neuhaus explains in his book that he put a stress on technique not in the usual sense but in the sense of the old Greek term τεχνε, which is more than just a form of mechanical practice to play a scale or a sequence of fast octaves.

Neuhaus reminds that this word actually means 'art,' which implies that any improvement of the technique, if done correctly, serves art, and not itself.

Thus, the understanding of a work of art and the technique involved in that process are intricately intertwined; this means that a brilliant performer cannot *not* care about technique, but at the same time the technique is never an end in itself, but serves art. He relates that when Richter played him Prokofiev's 9th piano sonata, which the composer dedicated to Richter, he could not help noticing that one very difficult, polyphonic and very lively bit … came off particularly well, so he asked Richter how he had managed to play these few hairy measures so well, and Richter had replied to him: 'I practiced this bit without interruption for two hours.'

Regarding Richter's hands, Neuhaus relates in *The Art of Piano Playing (1958/1973)* that Richter, while performing Chopin's *Polonaise-Fantasy*, had a clear advantage for rendering the final 47 measures after the both-hand scale up, where the melody, in this triumphant finale, is to be played forte and fortissimo with the forth and fifth finger while both hands are extremely busy with fast chord and octave play. Neuhaus writes that all pianists but those with huge hands had to 'cheat' here in one or the other way for coping with the strong tension in the hands.

A MAN OF DRAMA

This is a remark of my own, that I haven't found in any of the biographical material about Richter and is the impression I got of this man when facing him myself, back in 1982, during the Paris recital. I had a spontaneous association, when I saw him, with *Shakespeare* and was not surprised that he played Beethoven's Sonata, *The Tempest (op. 31/2)* so well, as this sonata is said to have been inspired by Shakespeare's drama of that same title.

I got a felt sense, when I saw Richter, that if he had not done a career in music, he would have become an actor. I was almost sure about it, and his way to walk onto the stage, and leave the stage was so unique, his way of bowing was so unusual, and the grace with which he took the flowers handed over to him after the recital was so natural that I couldn't help thinking that if this genius was not to become one in the musical world, he would have become a genius in theater and film. And in so far it's not a mere coincidence that he made his debut not as a prodigy pianist, but as a repetitor in the Odessa Opera House.

Richter had a strong talent also for the other arts and in this respect he was much more than a pianist, much more even than a musician. In my view, he was what in olden times was called a *man of letters;* this is how he came over to me in that encounter, as a true *philosopher*. I respectfully nicknamed him 'Socrates of the Piano.'

Chapter Five

The Genius of Keith Jarrett

General Remarks

The dichotomy of musical composition versus musical performance, so typical for our time of fragmentation, falls with Keith Jarrett. He went back in time, to connect with the pre-virtuoso tradition in which the composer was his own performer.

At that time, musical performance was different from what we know today. Composers played their own works and the works of other composers, and they *improvised* just as today Jazz musicians do.

— See Harold C. Schonberg, The Great Pianists: From Mozart to the Present, New York: Simon and Schuster (Fireside), 2006, first published in 1963, 128.

Bach improvised a lot. So did Beethoven. So did Mozart. They did not play in a mechanical and dry manner as so many pianists today understand their written music. They played so-called 'fantasies,' which were improvisations just as today Keith Jarrett's are. The only difference is perhaps that they wrote their improvisations down, while a score is, as Bach once voiced, already a 'transcription' of the original much more sophisticated improvisation.

And it's certainly not a coincidence that Keith Jarrett, besides being an outstanding Jazz musician, plays selected works by Bach, Handel, Mozart and Shostakovich, and his genius here in interpreting the old masters is not a minor one!

I have since my younger years discovered the amazing similarity between the figured bass—also called basso continuo—as the foundation of all Baroque music, and the quint cycle used in Jazz to do progressions and develop a theme in a virtuoso manner. As a matter of musical logic, then, it appears sound why Jarrett plays either Baroque music, or modern music, next to Jazz. In all these compositions, the same basic harmonic principles apply; while this is not always the case with Romantic music. There is thus an interconnecting intelligence between *Jarrett's Bach, Jarrett's Handel, Jarrett's Mozart, Jarrett's Shostakovich*, and *Jarrett's Jazz*. Jarrett has a very developed understanding of musical style. You can compare him with nobody. Who else, in human musical history, has been proficient to play both classical and Jazz with equal virtuosity?

In Jazz, one could compare Jarrett with Art Tatum and Oscar Peterson, but again, he is different. His Jazz is not African, it is rather Caucasian, using most unusual scales used by street violinists and wandering circus musicians in the Balkan. His Jazz is not 'black American,' nor 'white American,' it is Eastern European. This is, taken as such, already a rare feature in the Jazz world.

Then there are reminiscences of Bach, of Handel, of Shostakovich in his musical lines. Ultimately, Jarrett's Jazz is a fusion of classical and modern, and Jazz piano, an ingenuous mix, unmatched by any of his brothers in fate.

Jarrett and Inner Knowledge

To come back to our initial question, genius and inner knowledge—one could argue that what Picasso was in the visual arts, Jarrett is in music. He creates, and creates more. There is joy and abundance in his creations, there is an incredible, childlike, and almost hilarious *vitality* in his renderings of standards. And there is *novelty*. He masters all styles, and in one single rendering of a standard, he may switch styles three times.

It is obvious, when you listen to Jarrett, that such genius of melodic inventiveness, of amazing pianistry, and of spontaneous composition cannot be learnt. It is inborn, or rather the result of an inner continuum, a dimension of *inner knowledge* that is directly connected with the quantum field.

Many amateurs of his music will agree when I say there is *space* in his music, huge space, a vastness that cannot be put in words. To explain his unique gift with hereditary affiliation is a weak argument that was more or less proven wrong by genius research. As I have shown when discussing the genius of Einstein, genius is not hereditary. Einstein's parents had nothing about them that makes the world remember them. Remarks are rare that talk about Jarrett's origins. He usually is mentioned as an 'American' and a 'Christian' pianist, and wants to come over as such, apparently, when he plays tunes like *The Good America* or *God Bless the Child*. But that doesn't say anything about his musical identity. It well says something about his gratitude toward America, the country that helped him achieve success, glory and worldwide renown.

Jarrett's Shostakovich

Jarrett's Shostakovich is outstanding and novel. His musical vision of the *24 Preludes and Fugues,* op. 87 by Dimitri Shostakovich can stand against the rendering of any of our greatest classical pianists, if ever they have recorded the integral version at all. Most pianists, it is true, play a selection here, as for example Svjatoslav Richter.

Both Bach and Shostakovich have over time been recognized as musical geniuses, and both were most masterful in construing musical forms known as the 'Prelude' and the 'Fugue.' Both composers also have in common that they shared a musical philosophy that could be described as 'simplicity in complexity,' which is one of the reasons why their compositions are not easy to play.

While technically speaking the music does for the most part not require what may be called 'higher piano technique' as developed by Chopin, Liszt and Debussy, the difficulty for the performing musician lies in the accurate rendering of the musical lines that are often interwoven in a complex musical texture that needs a *bel canto* rendering of the main musical voices.

Jarrett seems to be a kin spirit to Shostakovich's; there is an intrinsic harmony between composition and expression. I would go as far as saying that no interpretation was needed here as it was obsolete.

Where there is a complete fusion between the composer's and performer's spirits, there is no more room for interpretation. Keith Jarrett surely is one of those pianists for whom the written score is sacred! And let me note also that Shostakovich's progression style, the way he progresses from one Prelude/Fugue pair to the next, differs from Bach's, as he does not progress chromatically but within the quint cycle, which is after all the progression cycle of the Jazzers.

PRELUDE AND FUGUE 1/24
C-MAJOR

This is a tender beginning, almost like a spring song, with this ethereal chord theme. This Prelude is all in piano and pianissimo, with one short forte passage toward the end. It's a very poetic beginning of the cycle. Jarrett plays this without weight, in a *sotto voce* style—and this is how it should.

The Fugue is a musical meditation, and this is a challenge for the pianist, as all those who are restless and impatient, and also those who want to show off are simply killed by such a piece.

In Bach's Well-Tempered Clavier there are several such meditative slow fugues, and most pianists appear to forget about the sound. I can't imagine who could play this fugue better than Jarrett, and how it should be played in any other way?

PRELUDE AND FUGUE 2/24
A-MINOR

The second Prelude is a jewel, a chain of pearls, a diamond, a luminescent glissando. Jarrett plays it as such, while I could imagine it would sound still very well when played a bit slower. But surely the speed adds on to the fantastic and luminous quality of this bizarre and exalted piece.

The Fugue is a real counterpoint to the Prelude in the sense that it's marked with syncopes, an academic example of a fugue in the old style. Jarrett renders it in such a brilliant, well-sounding and artistic manner that it does not come over as dry and pedantic. Perhaps when played by a lesser pianist, the bizarre beauty of this scurrilous piece could be easily lost.

PRELUDE AND FUGUE 3/24
G-MAJOR

The theme of the third Prelude reminds of Mussorgsky's *Pictures of an Exhibition*. It's a poetic piece with its pesante octaves in the left hand and its theme in the right hand that reminds of a fanfare, or a shrill announcement on a market fare—it's truly Russian. The atmosphere here is folkloristic.

The Fugue is in the same fantastic mood, exalted, poetic, Russian—and incredibly fast to play. Jarrett manages the staccatos to sound musical and not hard and dry; his rendering is all flesh and bones, with a good structure that seems to bounce off by itself. Incredible pianistry that expresses exactly what is written in the score—and this is how it should!

PRELUDE AND FUGUE 4/24
E-MINOR

The e-minor Prelude exhales the breath of deep loneliness, which perfectly fits the serious mood of this tonality. There is pain to be felt in the tight phrasings that are rendered with an admirable accuracy by Jarrett.

The Fugue is a wonderful piece of meditation, reminding of the most beautiful slow fugues of Johann Sebastian Bach. It's a piece that a show-off pianist will never even consider to play, let alone master. After a very slow and meditative introductory theme, a second theme comes up, which is a variation of the first, but that jubilates and rejoices.

This music is honest and religious. Jarrett shows here his true face, the face of an inspired, honest and religious musician. The purity of both the composer and the pianist coincide here in a wonderful way. This piece is a jewel!

PRELUDE AND FUGUE 5/24
D-MAJOR

The prelude is a pure wonder of musical genius, something I have never heard before in my life, and that truly transformed me. It strongly associates innocence, small children and fairy tales, which fits the serene D-major tonality. While the context is serious and meditative, we encounter here the pure joy of fairy life in its natural, genuine and unsentimental beauty. This childlike character is especially pronounced in the playful Fugue theme.

PRELUDE AND FUGUE 6/24
B-MINOR

Some of the Preludes and Fugues are obviously inspired by Bach's *Well-Tempered Clavier*. I mention this here, for this Prelude, exemplarily, in order to avoid being repetitive, as this is of course true for the entire collection. In fact, the b-minor Prelude is similar in style and gravity, with its punctuations, to Bach's Prelude XVI, BWV 885, from the 2nd Volume of the *Well-Tempered Clavier*, yet what Shostakovich makes out of similar style or musical patterns is extraordinary and shows his musical genius. He fills the space virtually with his own charm, his own tonal sensations, his own harmony changes, that are uncanny to a point that harmonic relationships are often difficult to make out. Jarrett plays this piece without the oft-heard exaggeration of the punctuations (which make them 'fall'). It's a real 'Allegretto,' which is indicated by Shostakovich and which traditionally asks for a rather fluent diction. Jarrett, again, has hit the point.

The Fugue is rendered by Jarrett in naturally intertwined melodies, very fluently, and without gravity.

PRELUDE AND FUGUE 7/24
A-MAJOR

This Prelude is pure heaven. While it reminds perhaps more than any other of Bach, it puts elements, little harmonious exaltations and changes that are real novelty and let appear this piece as angelic, childlike and light.

Jarrett's rendering accentuates the etheric nature of the piece, even more so for the Fugue, which is a true *Gloria in Excelsis Deo* in some way. It's as if listening to the angels sing in heaven. I can't find a better expression.

PRELUDE AND FUGUE 8/24
F-SHARP-MINOR

This Prelude reminds some of the fairy pieces we exercised so often in our first years of piano training. It's full of subtle humor, and expels an atmosphere of magic or spoke that fits so well the tonal realm of f sharp minor. Jarrett plays the *staccati* in a wonderfully light and fluent manner.

Now, the Fugue … well, I really have to say a word here. It's a very sad piece, more depressive than Bach's most depressive fugues, and it is terribly long and *gravissime* in character, with real sighs, put in music, an effect which is accentuated by the chromatic style of composition. It is like a day in Hell, reminding of Dante's *Inferno*, with burning flames all around and one's head put in ashes.

Fortunately Jarrett did not lighten up the bad mood but went through it, to render a piece that is truly cathartic in character. However, his genius was such that he avoided to get stuck in detail, resting fluent all through the piece. And his wonderful *bel canto* invites for listening to the admittedly beautiful melodic lines in the alto and the bass.

PRELUDE AND FUGUE 9/24
E-MAJOR

This Prelude is the strangest thing that I have ever heard. It's in luminous E-major but actually is 'felt' as being written in c-sharp-minor, and rather serious in character, a dialogue between two musical lines, one in the treble, one in the bass, a piece that is pianistically very ungrateful and obviously 'thought' of as orchestral by the composer.

The Fugue is a joyful and truly luminous piece that Jarrett plays very 'dense,' rendering thus in a unique manner the virtuosity of this composition, which would not sound as convincing in a slower tempo. Needless to add that to play this piece in the tempo Jarrett renders it, and in the flawlessness of his diction, shows that Jarrett can't be mingled with the crowd of ordinary pianists, much like Richter couldn't. Jarrett simply is great here, and unique.

PRELUDE AND FUGUE 10/24
C-SHARP-MINOR

This Prelude is another example for the obvious affiliation here with the Prelude VII in E-flat, BWV 852, from the First Volume of the *Well-Tempered Clavier*. But this regards only the starting motif, which is repeated over and over, while all the other style elements are novel.

Actually these reminiscences are by no means disturbing nor are they 'imitative' in character. I would say they are like poetic quotations, like a poet quoting an admired master poet, as a matter of reverence, and for rendering homage. As to the rendering of this piece, I find it again intelligent to play it in *leggerissimo* style, that Jarrett masters so well.

The Fugue is a 5-pages long contemplative piece, a true musical meditation, beautiful, religious, without gravity, angelic and heavenly serene.

This is perhaps one of the most beautiful compositions that Shostakovich enriched us with.

PRELUDE AND FUGUE 11/24
B-MAJOR

This Prelude in radiant b major reminds of Prokofiev; it is burlesque and poetic in character. It seems to be taken from a fairy world. Jarrett plays it with a wonderful finesse and accurate delicateness of touch and sound.

The Fugue is similar in character, but very fast, and as indicated by the composer, *marcatissimo*.

Jarrett's rendering simply is brilliant in every respect. And let me add here that this music is really not easy to play, contrary to what appears to be the case from a first look at the score.

PRELUDE AND FUGUE 12/24
G-SHARP-MINOR

This Prelude is truly a grave piece, not very agreeable to listen to, for my taste, as the composition is not very colorful, and Jarrett truly makes the best out of it, without getting too deep in the depressive mood of this very meditative piece.

The Fugue is quite opposite in character, marked with syncopes, and very dense in melodic structure.

I would never put my fingers on this piece of music as it's really difficult to render. Jarrett's take of this piece left me speechless and put the question in my mind why he ever played Jazz and did not dedicate his life to classical music? The answer is simply that his genius is greater, still greater.

PRELUDE AND FUGUE 13/24
F-SHARP-MAJOR

This Prelude seems to mark another cycle, as it's with the Second Volume of Bach's *Well-Tempered Clavier*. This Prelude is of a different kind altogether.

It's not Baroque in character and style, but Classical, something like an Impromptu. The character of the Prelude is serene, bathed in light, and it has a touch of Chopin.

The Fugue is meditative, calm, serene, and Jarrett renders the musical lines distinctly, with a melodic sense that I have hardly ever heard. Masterly rendering of this majestic opening of the second volume.

PRELUDE AND FUGUE 14/24
E-FLAT-MINOR

This Prelude is dramatic, Wagnerian in character, somber and sad, almost a background music to Shakespeare's *The Tempest*. In terms of style, it's truly amazing, as it uses the octave tremolo in the left hand, a technique that was to my knowledge never used in Baroque music, but was introduced in the pianistic vocabulary by Beethoven. It's overall a very exalted piece, painful that it hurts you under your skin, abrasive, bearing a note of some of Chopin's very dark Preludes.

Then, suddenly, a calmer resolve comes up shortly before the end, where the tension is quieted and the mood more tender. But it's spooky nonetheless, until the end.

The Fugue only increases the sadness with its almost fatalistic theme that gaily sings along, yet with a black heart, so to speak. The overall temper is depression, and Jarrett renders this piece with marvelous density and real color, as this Fugue is really colorful in the style of Olivier Messiaen.

PRELUDE AND FUGUE 15/24
D-FLAT-MAJOR

This Prelude is a dance. The theme sounds very popular, as if taken from folklore. It's gay, poetic, childlike, reminding of Prokofiev. Jarrett is a bit too 'dry' on the staccato octaves, for my taste.

The Fugue is one of the strangest musical pieces I have heard in my life. It is to be played in a *Molto Allegro* (1/4=188) and contains endless syncopes that require the pianist to get into a frenzy when swinging with the Gestalt of the piece.

This piece was majestically rendered by *Svjatoslav Richter,* in an early recording, and as an Encore. It appears as the dance of a madman, lunatic, extreme, exalted, ecstatic mind, reminding me strongly of Ravel's *Alborada Del Gracioso,* and as that unique piece of virtuoso pianistry, and in the tempo it should be played, it's achievable only for the chosen few of the best pianists in the world. It's perhaps the single most original piece of this entire collection.

PRELUDE AND FUGUE 16/24
B-FLAT-MINOR

This Prelude is Romantic in style, with beautiful musical lines that almost remind of Rachmaninov, but also of Bach. It's etheric, religious, passionate, and it really enchants, almost like a fairy dance.

The Fugue is beautiful, religion and purity translated in music, and every pianist can learn here from Jarrett's interpretation what *legatissimo* means, as marked by the composer, and to be held until the end. In this piece you clearly hear that one microphone was put inside of the grand piano, so as to render the hammer mechanics, the subtle sound of the felt dampers, and of the pedal. ECM has done, as always, a wonderful recording job in this collection, which was a gift not only for the pianist, but for all of us.

PRELUDE AND FUGUE 17/24
A-FLAT-MAJOR

This Prelude is a unique composition, expressing a joy I have heard before with no other composer and inspired by true innocence. The 'light touch' Jarrett has for this kind of childlike pieces really fits. Most pianists couldn't render this correctly, including Richter who is much too intense most of the time, instead of giving freedom to the musical lines. Unfortunately, Jarrett, when the theme comes with the thirds in the right hand, slightly accelerates, which is not sound from musical logic, but comes over as arbitrary.

The Fugue is like a post-script of the Prelude. I never heard anything of the kind. It's a true musical novelty. The Fugue is a smart continuation of the Prelude, however *dolce*, as it is indicated by the composer, a sweet interlace of musical lines, while extremely difficult to play because of staccato and legato being tightly interwoven in both hands—and that over 7 pages! I will never ever listen to another pianist playing this.

It's Jarrett's lively inner child that distinguishes him as a pianist, in a way so unique that I am unable to convey it with words. His unrivaled success may be an indication, but it's not. There are many other pianists who are successful but who do not have his level of genius. So what is it? I honestly think it's because he is not a pianist, but a composer, while a

Jazzer naturally does not consider himself a composer, but an *improviser.* Yet seen from the right perspective, the truth is that Jarrett has by far transcended Jazz piano and is to be considered as a composer.

PRELUDE AND FUGUE 18/24
F-MINOR

This Prelude is very peculiar in character. I would consider it as fragile: a wonderful melody unfolding in an intimate way.

Jarrett's rendering is pure genius. Without such sensitivity and extreme care in the voicings and purity of sound, the piece could easily be mistaken as trivial.

The Fugue is of the same vintage of purity, bearing a sense of wonder, and the texture is wonderfully dense and yet limpid and luminous.

PRELUDE AND FUGUE 19/24
E-FLAT-MAJOR

This Prelude is like a celebration, of a festive character, solemn like a hymn, and chromatic in the musical lines.

The Fugue is an example of chromatic lines, and I have never heard anything even remotely similar to this unique piece of music that is rather painful to hear, as the theme is so terribly dolorous, and depressive. Jarrett's rendering by far surpasses that of Svjatoslav Richter here, as he brings out parts of the texture in a true pianissimo, and then again lets the theme shine up, which makes it easier to listen to this Golgotha until the end.

PRELUDE AND FUGUE 20/24
C-MINOR

This Prelude is aloof, difficult to grasp, and very unusual as a composition. It's sad from the first to the last note. The Fugue is very 'Bach' in character, an intimate religious piece that comes over as just another catharsis after long and painful suffering. I cannot think of any other living pianist today who can render this piece at this level of musical genius.

Once more, Jarrett's grasp of this collection comes as a true blessing that will probably make musical history, and this so much the more as Shostakovich is still little known in our musical circles.

PRELUDE AND FUGUE 21/24
B-FLAT-MAJOR

This Prelude is a brilliant piece of pianistry, a toccata-like composition that sets the pianist in front of himself or herself. Jarrett's dexterity is beyond doubt as he plays this piece not Allegro, as indicated, but Presto. As such, the piece comes over as as pianistic *tour de force* that bears resemblance with Hungarian 'Gypsy' music, which also is often played in breath-taking tempi. Is it daring to say that Jarrett has recognized here some of his own cultural roots?

I want to see the pianist who can play this piece in the tempo Jarrett plays it, and with the same finesse and in a staggering non-legato!

The Fugue continues the toccata style; some passages convey a sense of drama, while the piece may sound rather academic on first approach.

PRELUDE AND FUGUE 22/24
G-MINOR

This Prelude is a Romantic piece that seems to express the composer's soul, intimate and 'Russian' in character, religious, in a serious, almost mystical mood, and with a sense of nobility.

The Fugue is serious, beautiful and religious and is overall soft and mellow, with some passages shining up in a glorious crescendo. Jarrett's piano and pianissimo is absolutely unheard of. Richter always said that the most difficult for the pianist is to play a true pianissimo; ironically so, he himself was not really able to: many pieces played by him in his earlier years are spoilt simply because he played them too loud, and too 'affirmative' in style, with too much personality. While Jarrett is pretty much the opposite character, and that really pays in this collection.

PRELUDE AND FUGUE 23/24
F-MAJOR

This Prelude is a melodic piece, noble in character, serene and really romantic, poetic and tender in its general expression. The Fugue is like playing children and their joy and playfulness transformed into music. A wonderful innocence shines through, an innocent heart and soul. It's a wonderful piece of music yet very difficult to play in the take that Jarrett made of it.

PRELUDE AND FUGUE 24/24
D-MINOR

This Prelude is a majestic composition, rather traditional in its overall character, as if composed for a festive solemn occasion, gloriously finalizing the collection.

Unfortunately this Prelude and Fugue are recorded in a different set and setting. The overall recording volume is markedly lower and the microphone seems to be placed in a greater distance to the piano which spoils much of the charm.

The 8-pages Fugue is a true monster, sad, convoluted, perhaps the expression of an endless stream of thoughts. Jarrett really makes the best out of it.

This is dry music, lacking color from the very core of the composition, so much the more as the recording quality does not match the one in the other pieces. But it could also be that this was a choice made by Jarrett, or by the producer, because there are extreme fortissimo passages in this Fugue that might have caused problems with recording dynamics and peak levels when using the same recording technology as chosen for the other pieces.

This is for any pianist a very ungrateful piece to render. Jarrett is beyond the little critter and transforms this musical monster into a majestic and turbulent ending of the cycle.

Bibliography
Contextual Bibliography

Abrams, Jeremiah (Ed.)
Reclaiming the Inner Child
New York: Tarcher/Putnam, 1990

Arntz, William & Chasse, Betsy
What the Bleep Do We Know
20th Century Fox, 2005 (DVD)

Down The Rabbit Hole Quantum Edition
20th Century Fox, 2006 (3 DVD Set)

Assagioli, Roberto
Psychosynthesis
A Collection of Basic Writings
New York: Synthesis Center, 2000
First published in 1965

Bateson, Gregory
Steps to an Ecology of Mind
Chicago: University of Chicago Press, 2000
Originally published in 1972

Besant, Annie
An Autobiography
New Delhi: Penguin Books, 2005
Originally published in 1893

Blavatsky, Helena Petrovna

The Secret Doctrine
New York: Tarcher, 2009
Originally published in 1888

Bohm, David

Wholeness and the Implicate Order
London: Routledge, 2002

Thought as a System
London: Routledge, 1994

Quantum Theory
London: Dover Publications, 1989

Brennan, Barbara Ann

Hands of Light
A Guide to Healing Through the Human Energy Field
New York: Bantam Books, 1988

Burwick, Frederick

The Damnation of Newton
Goethe's Color Theory and Romantic Perception
New York: Walter de Gruyter, 1986

Campbell, Herbert James

The Pleasure Areas
London: Eyre Methuen Ltd., 1973

Campbell, Joseph

The Hero With A Thousand Faces
Princeton: Princeton University Press, 1973 (Bollingen Series XVII)
London: Orion Books, 1999

Occidental Mythology
Princeton: Princeton University Press, 1973
(Bollingen Series XVII)
New York: Penguin Arkana, 1991
The Masks of God
Oriental Mythology
New York: Penguin Arkana, 1992
Originally published in 1962

The Power of Myth
With Bill Moyers
ed. by Sue Flowers
New York: Anchor Books, 1988

Capra, Fritjof

The Tao of Physics
An Exploration of the Parallels Between Modern
Physics and Eastern Mysticism
New York: Shambhala Publications, 2000
(New Edition) Originally published in 1975

The Turning Point
Science, Society And The Rising Culture
New York: Simon & Schuster, 1987 (Author Copyright 1982)

Green Politics
With Charlene Spretnak
Rochester, VT: Inner Traditions, 1986

The Web of Life
A New Scientific Understanding of Living Systems
New York: Doubleday, 1997
Author Copyright 1996

The Hidden Connections
Integrating The Biological, Cognitive And Social
Dimensions Of Life Into A Science Of Sustainability
New York: Doubleday, 2002

Steering Business Toward Sustainability
New York: United Nations University Press, 1995
Uncommon Wisdom
Conversations with Remarkable People
New York: Bantam, 1989

The Science of Leonardo
Inside the Mind of the Great Genius of the Renaissance
New York: Anchor Books, 2008
New York: Bantam Doubleday, 2007 (First Publishing)

Learning from Leonardo
Decoding the Notebooks of a Genius
San Francisco: Berrett-Koehler, 2013

Carnegie, Dale

How to Win Friends and Influence People
The Only Book You Need to Lead You to Success
New York: Pocket Books, 1998
First published in 1937

Chaplin, Charles

My Autobiography
New York: Plume, 1992
Originally published in 1964

Chopra, Deepak

Creating Affluence
The A-to-Z Steps to a Richer Life
New York: Amber-Allen Publishing (2003)

Synchrodestiny
Discover the Power of Meaningful Coincidence to Manifest Abundance
Audio Book / CD
Niles, IL: Nightingale-Conant, 2006

The Seven Spiritual Laws of Success
A Practical Guide to the Fulfillment of Your Dreams
Audio Book / CD
New York: Amber-Allen Publishing (2002)

The Spontaneous Fulfillment of Desire
Harnessing the Infinite Power of Coincidence
New York: Random House Audio, 2003

Clarke, Ronald

Einstein: The Life and Times
New York: Avon Books, 1970

Constantine, Larry L.

Children & Sex
New Findings, New Perspectives
Larry L. Constantine & Floyd M. Martinson (Eds.)
Boston: Little, Brown & Company, 1981

Treasures of the Island
Children in Alternative Lifestyles
Beverly Hills: Sage Publications, 1976

Where are the Kids?
in: Libby & Whitehurst (ed.)
Marriage and Alternatives
Glenview: Scott Foresman, 1977

Currier, Richard L.
Juvenile Sexuality in Global Perspective
in : Children & Sex, New Findings, New Perspectives
Larry L. Constantine & Floyd M. Martinson (Eds.)
Boston: Little, Brown & Company, 1981

De Bono, Edward
The Use of Lateral Thinking
New York: Penguin, 1967

The Mechanism of Mind
New York: Penguin, 1969

Sur/Petition
London: HarperCollins, 1993

Tactics
London: HarperCollins, 1993
First published in 1985

Serious Creativity
Using the Power of Lateral Thinking to Create New Ideas
London: HarperCollins, 1996

DeMause, Lloyd
The History of Childhood
New York, 1974

Foundations of Psychohistory
New York: Creative Roots, 1982

DeMeo, James
Heretic's Notebook
Emotions, Protocells, Ether-Drift and Cosmic Life Energy
with New Research Supporting Wilhelm Reich
Pulse of the Planet, #5 (2002)
Ashland, Oregon: Orgone Biophysical Research Laboratories, Inc., 2002

DiCarlo, Russell E. (Ed.)

Towards A New World View
Conversations at the Leading Edge
Erie, PA: Epic Publishing, 1996

Dolto, Françoise

La Cause des Enfants
Paris: Laffont, 1985

Psychanalyse et Pédiatrie
Paris: Seuil, 1971

Séminaire de Psychanalyse d'Enfants, 1
Paris: Seuil, 1982

Séminaire de Psychanalyse d'Enfants, 2
Paris: Seuil, 1985

Séminaire de Psychanalyse d'Enfants, 3
Paris: Seuil, 1988

Dossey, Larry

Recovering the Soul
A Scientific and Spiritual Approach
New York: Bantam Books, 1989

Dürckheim, Karlfried Graf

Hara: The Vital Center of Man
Rochester: Inner Traditions, 2004

The Call for the Master
New York: Penguin Books, 1993

Absolute Living
The Otherworldly in the World and the Path to Maturity
New York: Penguin Arkana, 1992

The Way of Transformation
Daily Life as a Spiritual Exercise
London: Allen & Unwin, 1988

The Japanese Cult of Tranquility
London: Rider, 1960

Einstein, Albert

The World As I See It
New York: Citadel Press, 1993

Out of My Later Years
New York: Outlet, 1993

Ideas and Opinions
New York: Bonanza Books, 1988

Albert Einstein Notebook
London: Dover Publications, 1989

Emerson, Ralph Waldo

The Essays of Ralph Waldo Emerson
Cambridge, Mass.: Harvard University Press, 1987

Emoto, Masaru

The Hidden Messages in Water
New York: Atria Books, 2004

The Secret Life of Water
New York: Atria Books, 2005

Erickson, Milton H.

My Voice Will Go With You
The Teaching Tales of Milton H. Erickson
by Sidney Rosen (Ed.)
New York: Norton & Co., 1991

Complete Works 1.0, CD-ROM
New York: Milton H. Erickson Foundation, 2001

Erikson, Erik H.

Childhood and Society
New York: Norton, 1993
First published in 1950

Finkelstein, Haim N. (Ed.)

The Collected Writings of Salvador Dali
Cambridge: Cambridge University Press, 1998

Freud, Sigmund

Totem and Taboo
New York: Routledge, 1999
Originally published in 1913

Fromm, Erich

The Anatomy of Human Destructiveness
New York: Owl Book, 1992
Originally published in 1973

Escape from Freedom
New York: Owl Books, 1994
Originally published in 1941

To Have or To Be
New York: Continuum International Publishing, 1996
Originally published in 1976

The Art of Loving
New York: HarperPerennial, 2000
Originally published in 1956

Goethe, Johann Wolfgang von

The Theory of Colors
New York: MIT Press, 1970
First published in 1810

Goldenstein, Joyce

Einstein: Physicist and Genius
(Great Minds of Science)
New York: Enslow Publishers, 1995

Goldman, Jonathan & Goldman, Andi

Tantra of Sound
Frequencies of Healing
Charlottesville: Hampton Roads, 2005

Healing Sounds
The Power of Harmonies
Rochester: Healing Arts Press, 2002

Healing Sounds
Principles of Sound Healing
DVD, 90 min.

Sacred Mysteries, 2004

Grof, Stanislav
Ancient Wisdom and Modern Science
New York: State University of New York Press, 1984

Beyond the Brain
Birth, Death and Transcendence in Psychotherapy
New York: State University of New York, 1985

LSD: Doorway to the Numinous
The Groundbreaking Psychedelic Research into Realms of the Human
Unconscious
Rochester: Park Street Press, 2009

Realms of the Human Unconscious
Observations from LSD Research
New York: E.P. Dutton, 1976

The Cosmic Game
Explorations of the Frontiers of Human Consciousness
New York: State University of New York Press, 1998

The Holotropic Mind
The Three Levels of Human Consciousness
With Hal Zina Bennett
New York: HarperCollins, 1993

When the Impossible Happens
Adventures in Non-Ordinary Reality
Louisville, CO: Sounds True, 2005

Hall, Manly P.
The Secret Teachings of All Ages
Reader's Edition
New York: Tarcher/Penguin, 2003
Originally published in 1928

Hasegawa, Tsuyoshi
Racing the Enemy
Stalin, Truman, and the Surrender of Japan
Cambridge, MA: Belknap Press of Harvard University Press, 2006

Holmes, Ernest

The Science of Mind
A Philosophy, A Faith, A Way of Life
New York: Jeremy P. Tarcher/Putnam, 1998
First Published in 1938

Huxley, Aldous

The Doors of Perception and Heaven and Hell
London: HarperCollins (Flamingo), 1994
(originally published in 1954)

The Perennial Philosophy
San Francisco: Harper & Row, 1970

Jung, Carl Gustav

Archetypes of the Collective Unconscious
in: The Basic Writings of C.G. Jung
New York: The Modern Library, 1959, 358-407

Collected Works
New York, 1959

On the Nature of the Psyche
in: The Basic Writings of C.G. Jung
New York: The Modern Library, 1959, 47-133

Psychological Types
Collected Writings, Vol. 6
Princeton: Princeton University Press, 1971

Psychology and Religion
in: The Basic Writings of C.G. Jung
New York: The Modern Library, 1959, 582-655

Religious and Psychological Problems of Alchemy
in: The Basic Writings of C.G. Jung
New York: The Modern Library, 1959, 537-581

The Basic Writings of C.G. Jung
New York: The Modern Library, 1959

The Development of Personality
Collected Writings, Vol. 17
Princeton: Princeton University Press, 1954

The Meaning and Significance of Dreams
Boston: Sigo Press, 1991

The Myth of the Divine Child
in: Essays on A Science of Mythology
Princeton, N.J.: Princeton University Press Bollingen
Series XXII, 1969. (With Karl Kerenyi)

Two Essays on Analytical Psychology
Collected Writings, Vol. 7
Princeton: Princeton University Press, 1972
First published by Routledge & Kegan Paul, Ltd., 1953

Krishnamurti, J.

Freedom From The Known
San Francisco: Harper & Row, 1969

The First and Last Freedom
San Francisco: Harper & Row, 1975

Education and the Significance of Life
London: Victor Gollancz, 1978

Commentaries on Living
First Series
London: Victor Gollancz, 1985

Commentaries on Living
Second Series
London: Victor Gollancz, 1986

Krishnamurti's Journal
London: Victor Gollancz, 1987

Krishnamurti's Notebook
London: Victor Gollancz, 1986

Beyond Violence
London: Victor Gollancz, 1985

Beginnings of Learning
New York: Penguin, 1986

The Penguin Krishnamurti Reader
New York: Penguin, 1987

On God
San Francisco: Harper & Row, 1992

On Fear
San Francisco: Harper & Row, 1995

The Essential Krishnamurti
San Francisco: Harper & Row, 1996

The Ending of Time
With Dr. David Bohm
San Francisco: Harper & Row, 1985

LaBerge, Stephen

Exploring the World of Lucid Dreaming
With Howard Rheingold
New York: Ballantine Books, 1991

Lakhovsky, Georges

Secret of Life
New York: Kessinger Publishing, 2003

Lanouette, William

Genius in the Shadows
A Biography of Leo Szilard, the Man behind the Bomb
With Bela Silard
Chicago: University of Chicago Press, 1994

Laszlo, Ervin

Science and the Akashic Field
An Integral Theory of Everything
Rochester: Inner Traditions, 2004

Quantum Shift to the Global Brain
How the New Scientific Reality Can Change Us and Our World
Rochester: Inner Traditions, 2008

Science and the Reenchantment of the Cosmos
The Rise of the Integral Vision of Reality
Rochester: Inner Traditions, 2006

The Akashic Experience
Science and the Cosmic Memory Field
Rochester: Inner Traditions, 2009

The Chaos Point
The World at the Crossroads
Newburyport, MA: Hampton Roads Publishing, 2006

LaViolette, Paul A.
Secrets of Antigravity Propulsion: Tesla, UFOs, and Classified Aerospace Technology
New York: Bear & Company, 2008

The U.S. Antigravity Squadron
In: Thomas Valone, Ed., *Electrogravitics Systems,*
Reports on a New Propulsion Methodology
Washington, D.C.: Integrity Research Institute, 1993, 78-96

Leadbeater, Charles Webster
Astral Plane
Its Scenery, Inhabitants and Phenomena
Kessinger Publishing Reprint Edition, 1997

Dreams
What they Are and How they are Caused
London: Theosophical Publishing Society, 1903
Kessinger Publishing Reprint Edition, 1998

The Inner Life
Chicago: The Rajput Press, 1911
Kessinger Publishing

Leary Timothy
Your Brain is God
Berkeley, CA: Ronin Publishing, 2001

Leboyer, Frederick
Birth Without Violence
New York, 1975

Inner Beauty, Inner Light
New York: Newmarket Press, 1997

Loving Hands
The Traditional Art of Baby Massage
New York: Newmarket Press, 1977

The Art of Breathing
New York: Newmarket Press, 1991

Liedloff, Jean
Continuum Concept
In Search of Happiness Lost
New York: Perseus Books, 1986
First published in 1977

Long, Max
The Secret Science at Work
The Huna Method as a Way of Life
Marina del Rey: De Vorss Publications, 1995
Originally published in 1953

Growing Into Light
A Personal Guide to Practicing the Huna Method,
Marina del Rey: De Vorss Publications, 1955

Lowen, Alexander
Bioenergetics
New York: Coward, McGoegham 1975

Depression and the Body
The Biological Basis of Faith and Reality
New York: Penguin, 1992

Fear of Life
New York: Bioenergetic Press, 2003

Honoring the Body
The Autobiography of Alexander Lowen
New York: Bioenergetic Press, 2004

Joy
The Surrender to the Body and to Life
New York: Penguin, 1995

Love and Orgasm
New York: Macmillan, 1965

Love, Sex and Your Heart
New York: Bioenergetics Press, 2004

Narcissism: Denial of the True Self
New York: Macmillan, Collier Books, 1983

Pleasure: A Creative Approach to Life
New York: Bioenergetics Press, 2004
First published in 1970

The Language of the Body
Physical Dynamics of Character Structure
New York: Bioenergetics Press, 2006
First published in 1958

Maharshi, Ramana
The Collected Works of Ramana Maharshi
New York: Sri Ramanasramam, 2002

The Essential Teachings of Ramana Maharshi
A Visual Journey
New York: Inner Directions Publishing, 2002
by Matthew Greenblad

Malinowski, Bronislaw
Crime und Custom in Savage Society
London: Kegan, 1926

Sex and Repression in Savage Society
London: Kegan, 1927
The Sexual Life of Savages in North West Melanesia
New York: Halcyon House, 1929

Martinson, Floyd M.
Sexual Knowledge
Values and Behavior Patterns
St. Peter: Minn.: Gustavus Adolphus College, 1966

Infant and Child Sexuality
St. Peter: Minn.: Gustavus Adolphus College, 1973

The Quality of Adolescent Experiences
St. Peter: Minn.: Gustavus Adolphus College, 1974

The Child and the Family
Calgary, Alberta: The University of Calgary, 1980

The Sex Education of Young Children
in: Lorna Brown (Ed.), *Sex Education in the Eighties*
New York, London: Plenum Press, 1981, pp. 51 ff.

The Sexual Life of Children
New York: Bergin & Garvey, 1994

Children and Sex, Part II: Childhood Sexuality
in: Bullough & Bullough, Human Sexuality (1994)
Pp. 111-116

McTaggart, Lynne
The Field
The Quest for the Secret Force of the Universe
New York: Harper & Collins, 2002

Mead, Margaret
Sex and Temperament in Three Primitive Societies
New York, 1935

Metzner, Ralph (Ed.)
Ayahuasca, Human Consciousness and the Spirits of Nature
ed. by Ralph Metzner, Ph.D
New York: Thunder's Mouth Press, 1999

The Psychedelic Experience
A Manual Based on the Tibetan Book of the Dead
With Timothy Leary and Richard Alpert
New York: Citadel, 1995

Miller, Alice
Four Your Own Good
Hidden Cruelty in Child-Rearing and the Roots of Violence
New York: Farrar, Straus & Giroux, 1983

Pictures of a Childhood
New York: Farrar, Straus & Giroux, 1986

The Drama of the Gifted Child
In Search for the True Self
translated by Ruth Ward
New York: Basic Books, 1996

Thou Shalt Not Be Aware
Society's Betrayal of the Child
New York: Noonday, 1998

Monsaingeon, Bruno

Svjatoslav Richter
Notebooks and Conversations
Princeton: Princeton University Press, 2002

Richter The Enigma / L'Insoumis / Der Unbeugsame
NVC Arts 1998 (DVD)

Montagu, Ashley

Touching
The Human Significance of the Skin
New York: Harper & Row, 1978

Moore, Thomas

Care of the Soul
A Guide for Cultivating Depth and Sacredness in Everyday Life
New York: Harper & Collins, 1994

Murphy, Joseph

The Power of Your Subconscious Mind
West Nyack, N.Y.: Parker, 1981, N.Y.: Bantam, 1982
Originally published in 1962

The Miracle of Mind Dynamics
New York: Prentice Hall, 1964

Miracle Power for Infinite Riches
West Nyack, N.Y.: Parker, 1972

The Amazing Laws of Cosmic Mind Power
West Nyack, N.Y.: Parker, 1973

Secrets of the I Ching
West Nyack, N.Y.: Parker, 1970

Think Yourself Rich
Use the Power of Your Subconscious Mind to Find True Wealth
Revised by Ian D. McMahan, Ph.D.
Paramus, NJ: Reward Books, 2001

Murphy, Michael

The Future of the Body
Explorations into the Further Evolution of Human Nature
New York: Jeremy P. Tarcher/Putnam, 1992

Nau, Erika

Self-Awareness Through Huna
Virginia Beach: Donning, 1981

Neuhaus, Heinrich

The Art of Piano Playing
London: Barrie & Jenkins, 1973
First published in 1958

Neill, Alexander Sutherland

Neill! Neill! Orange-Peel!
New York: Hart Publishing Co., 1972

Summerhill
A Radical Approach to Child Rearing
New York: Hart Publishing, Reprint 1984
Originally published in 1960

Summerhill School
A New View of Childhood
New York: St. Martin's Press
Reprint 1995

Newton, Michael

Life Between Lives
Hypnotherapy for Spiritual Regression
Woodbury, Minn.: Llewellyn Publications, 2006

Nichols, Sallie

Jung and Tarot: An Archetypal Journey
New York: Red Wheel/Weiser, 1986

Odent, Michel

Birth Reborn
What Childbirth Should Be
London: Souvenir Press, 1994

The Scientification of Love
London: Free Association Books, 1999

Primal Health
Understanding the Critical Period Between Conception and the First
Birthday
London: Clairview Books, 2002
First Published in 1986 with Century Hutchinson in London

The Functions of the Orgasms
The Highway to Transcendence
London: Pinter & Martin, 2009

Ong, Hean-Tatt

Amazing Scientific Basis of Feng-Shui
Kuala Lumpur: Eastern Dragon Press, 1997

Ostrander, Sheila & Schroeder, Lynn

Superlearning 2000
New York: Delacorte Press, 1994

Supermemory
New York: Carroll & Graf, 1991

Pert, Candace B.

Molecules of Emotion
The Science Behind Mind-Body Medicine
New York: Scribner, 2003

Ponder, Catherine

The Healing Secrets of the Ages
Marine del Rey: DeVorss, 1985

Prescott, James W.

Affectional Bonding for the Prevention of Violent Behaviors
Neurobiological, Psychological and Religious/Spiritual Determinants
in: Hertzberg, L.J., Ostrum, G.F. and Field, J.R., (Eds.)

Violent Behavior
Vol. 1, Assessment & Intervention, Chapter Six
New York: PMA Publishing, 1990

Alienation of Affection
Psychology Today, December 1979

Body Pleasure and the Origins of Violence
Bulletin of the Atomic Scientists, 10-20 (1975)
Deprivation of Physical Affection as a Primary Process in the
Development of Physical Violence
A Comparative and Cross-Cultural Perspective,
in: David G. Gil, ed., *Child Abuse and Violence*
New York: Ams Press, 1979

Early somatosensory deprivation as an ontogenetic process in the abnormal
development of the brain and behavior,
in: Medical Primatology, ed. by I.E. Goldsmith and J. Moor-Jankowski,
New York: S. Karger, 1971

Phylogenetic and ontogenetic aspects of human affectional
development, in: Progress in Sexology, Proceedings of the 1976
International Congress of Sexology, ed. by R. Gemme & C.C. Wheeler
New York: Plenum Press, 1977

Prevention or Therapy and the Politics of Trust
Inspiring a New Human Agenda
in: *Psychotherapy and Politics International*
Volume 3(3), pp. 194-211
London: John Wiley, 2005

Somatosensory affectional deprivation (SAD) theory of drug and alcohol use,
in: Theories on Drug Abuse: Selected Contemporary Perspectives,
ed. by Dan J. Lettieri, Mollie Sayers and Helen Wallenstien Pearson,
NIDA Research Monograph 30, March 1980
Rockville, MD: National Institute on Drug Abuse, Department of Health
and Human
Services, 1980

The Origins of Human Love and Violence
Pre- and Perinatal Psychology Journal
Volume 10, Number 3:
Spring 1996, pp. 143-188The Origins of Love and Violence
Sensory Deprivation and the Developing Brain
Research and Prevention (DVD)

Radin, Dean

The Conscious Universe
The Scientific Truth of Psychic Phenomena
San Francisco: Harper & Row, 1997

Entangled Minds
Extrasensory Experiences in a Quantum Reality
New York: Paraview Pocket Books, 2006

Raknes, Ola
Wilhelm Reich and Orgonomy
Oslo: Universitetsforlaget, 1970

Reich, Wilhelm
Children of the Future
On the Prevention of Sexual Pathology
New York: Farrar, Straus & Giroux, 1983
First published in 1950

CORE (Cosmic Orgone Engineering)
Part I, Space Ships, DOR and DROUGHT
©1984, Orgone Institute Press
XEROX Copy from the Wilhelm Reich Museum

Early Writings 1
New York: Farrar, Straus & Giroux, 1975

Ether, God & Devil & Cosmic Superimposition
New York: Farrar, Straus & Giroux, 1972
Originally published in 1949

Genitality in the Theory and Therapy of Neurosis
©1980 by Mary Boyd Higgins as Director of the Wilhelm Reich Infant
Trust

People in Trouble
©1974 by Mary Boyd Higgins as Director of the Wilhelm Reich Infant
Trust

Record of a Friendship
The Correspondence of Wilhelm Reich and A. S. Neill
New York, Farrar, Straus & Giroux, 1981

Selected Writings
An Introduction to Orgonomy
New York: Farrar, Straus & Giroux, 1973

The Bioelectrical Investigation of Sexuality and Anxiety
New York: Farrar, Straus & Giroux, 1983
Originally published in 1935

The Bion Experiments
reprinted in *Selected Writings*
New York: Farrar, Straus & Giroux, 1973

The Cancer Biopathy (The Orgone, Vol. 2)
New York: Farrar, Straus & Giroux, 1973

The Function of the Orgasm (The Orgone, Vol. 1)
Orgone Institute Press, New York, 1942

The Invasion of Compulsory Sex Morality
New York: Farrar, Straus & Giroux, 1971
Originally published in 1932

The Leukemia Problem: Approach
©1951, Orgone Institute Press
Copyright Renewed 1979
XEROX Copy from the Wilhelm Reich Museum

The Mass Psychology of Fascism
New York: Farrar, Straus & Giroux, 1970
Originally published in 1933

The Orgone Energy Accumulator
Its Scientific and Medical Use
©1951, 1979, Orgone Institute Press
XEROX Copy from the Wilhelm Reich Museum

The Schizophrenic Split
©1945, 1949, 1972 by Mary Boyd Higgins as Director of the
Wilhelm Reich Infant Trust
XEROX Copy from the Wilhelm Reich Museum

The Sexual Revolution
©1945, 1962 by Mary Boyd Higgins as Director of the Wilhelm Reich
Infant Trust

Rhodes, Richard
The Making of the Atomic Bomb
New York, Simon & Schuster, 1995

Schlipp, Paul A. (Ed.)
Albert Einstein
Philosopher-Scientist
New York: Open Court Publishing, 1988

Schonberg, Harold C.
The Great Pianists: From Mozart to the Present
New York: Simon and Schuster (Fireside), 2006
First published in 1963

Schultes, Richard Evans, et al.
Plants of the Gods
Their Sacred, Healing, and Hallucinogenic Powers
New York: Healing Arts Press
2nd edition, 2002

Sharaf, Myron
Fury on Earth
A Biography of Wilhelm Reich
London: André Deutsch, 1983

Sheldrake, Rupert
A New Science of Life
The Hypothesis of Morphic Resonance
Rochester: Park Street Press, 1995

Simonton, Otto Carl et al.
Getting Well Again
Los Angeles: Tarcher, 1978

Small, Jacquelyn
The Sacred Purpose of Being Human
A Journey Through the 12 Principles of Wholeness
New York: HCI, 2005

Stone, Hal & Stone, Sidra
Embracing Our Selves
The Voice Dialogue Manual
San Rafael, CA: New World Library, 1989

Strassman, Rick
DMT: The Spirit Molecule
A doctor's revolutionary research into the biology of near-death
and mystical experiences
Rochester: Park Street Press, 2001

Talbot, Michael

The Holographic Universe
New York: HarperCollins, 1992

Tatar, Maria M.

Spellbound: Studies on Mesmerism and Literature
Princeton, N.Y., 1978

Tiller, William A.

Conscious Acts of Creation
The Emergence of a New Physics
Associated Producers, 2004 (DVD)

Psychoenergetic Science
New York: Pavior, 2007

Conscious Acts of Creation
New York: Pavior, 2001

Wilber, Ken

Sex, Ecology, Spirituality
The Spirit of Evolution
Boston: Shambhala, 2000

Quantum Questions
Mystical Writings of The World's Greatest Physicists
Boston: Shambhala, 2001

Zyman, Sergio

The End of Marketing as We Know It
New York: HarperCollins, 2000

Personal Notes